edication

Angels are everywhere! And this book is dedicated to an angel named Ruth Arent, an internationally known author of books and wall charts on the subject of stress in adults and children.

It was Ruth who inspired the writing of this work, trusted my skills, knowledge and abilities and spent countless hours coaching, reading, challenging and supporting me. She helped me organize my thoughts and offered advice, guidance and encouragement—she believed in me!

Ruth was my number one cheerleader and the angel on my shoulder as I worked to pull all the pieces of this book together. I will forever admire her tenacity. I love her and thank her for sharing so much of herself with me.

Beyond *"Hello"*

A Practical Guide For Excellent Telephone Communication and Quality Customer Service

by
Jeannie Davis

edited by
Pat Landaker

Now Hear This, Inc. Publishing

Beyond "Hello"

by Jeannie Davis

Copyright ©2003 - Third printing

Now Hear This, Inc.
Printed in the United States
First Edition 1999

Now Hear This, Inc. Publishing
14571 E. Mississippi Avenue, Suite 213
Aurora, Colorado 80012
(303) 337-1991 or 1-800-784-5525
Fax: (303) 337-1966
Email: jeannie@phoneskills.com
Website: www.phoneskills.com

Library of Congress Catalog Card Number: 98-88128

ISBN Number: 0-944918-04-2

Cover/Layout Design by ORBIT Design
2560 Sheridan Blvd., Suite #4, Denver, CO 80214
(303) 433-1616

Edited by Pat Landaker

Acknowledgements

Thank you, Chuck! There's a lot to be said for loving relationships that really stand the test of time. Every hour, minute and second spent writing this book deprived us of valuable time together and I appreciate your thoughtfulness, understanding and patience.

I also want to thank the many relatives, friends and acquaintances who tolerated my absence from their lives and respected my need to concentrate and focus on this endeavor. Your willingness to engage in one-sided conversations, review bits and pieces of original drafts and provide truthful feedback is greatly appreciated!

And to those who said, "I bet you won't do this again"—bet me!

Thank you all.

Table of Contents

Foreword   **First Impressions Are Nine-Tenths of Reality**........................IX

Chapter 1   **Attitude: Now You Hear It—Now You Don't** 1
                     Put A Smile In Your Voice 2
                     Look Good To Yourself 4
                     Develop A "Can-Do" Attitude 7
                     Create Mutual Reliance 13

Chapter 2   **How To Say "Hello": Guidelines For Professional Greetings** 15
                     Offer A Salutation 16
                     State Your Company Name 17
                     State Your Department Name 18
                     Give Your Name 19
                     Offer Assistance 20

Chapter 3   **Call Screening And Probing: Getting The Information You Need**............27
                     Call-Screening Options 27
                     Probing Types 32

Chapter 4   **Call Transfer And Holding: Handling Calls Like A Pro** 39
                     Transferring Calls...39
                     Hold The Line 44

Chapter 5   **Messaging: The Give And Take Of It** 53
                     The Fine Art Of Message Taking 53
                     Avoid Awkward Responses 60

Chapter 6   **Voice Messaging: A Condiment For Business Success**............................65
                     Using Your Voice Messaging System 67
                     Leaving A Voice Mail Message 73

Chapter 7   **Handling Complaint Callers: Profit Opportunities With A Twist** 81
                Corporate Commitment 84
                Behavior Styles 85
                Climbing The Mountain of Anger 90
                Complaint Call Strategy 98

Chapter 8   **Painting A Self Portrait: How Do Your Customers PICTURE You?** 101
                Posture 103
                Inflection..105
                Courtesy 107
                Tone 110
                Understandability 114
                Rate of Speech 116
                Extra Mile 117

Chapter 9   **Communication Styles: Speaking Your Customer's Language** 121
                Communication Input and Output..122
                Speaking Your Customer's Language 123
                Identifying Communication Styles 125
                Matching Communication Styles 128

Chapter 10   **Now Hear This: Hearing Is Not Listening!** 131
                Ten Tips for Active Listening 132
                Five Common Barriers to Listening 140
                Encouraging Customers to Listen 143

In Summary   **Communication Is The Key**...145

Foreword

"First impressions are indelibly marked on the fabric of the mind."
– John J. Tarrant

First Impressions Are Nine-Tenths Of Reality

When you meet someone face-to-face, your appearance will determine the impression you make. Many people appear confident on the telephone because they don't have to worry about the visual image they're presenting. However, there are advantages and disadvantages to communicating via the telephone because while certain characteristics are disclosed others remain invisible. This is why it's important to present as complete a picture of yourself as possible when working on the telephone.

First impressions are difficult to achieve when only our audible senses are at work. You communicate at about 40% of your ability when on the telephone because your facial expressions and gesticulations can't be seen. Yet, there are many characteristics that do come across. To effectively create a good first impression on the telephone, you need to be aware of these characteristics.

People do form an opinion of you based on the way you present yourself on the telephone. Though you appreciate the anonymity this medium presents, you still must be aware of the image you're projecting. I've asked clients and workshop participants to identify characteristics they feel help make a good impression when meeting someone face-to-face. It's no surprise that appearance and attitude are among the first on the list.

Responses include the following characteristics:

Appearance	Articulate	Attentiveness
Attitude	Body Language	Confidence
Courteousness	Demeanor	Eye Contact
Friendliness	Good Listener	Greeting
Handshake	Helpfulness	Informative
Name	Pleasantness	Posture
Rate of Speech	Recall Ability	Responsiveness
Sincerity	Smile	Vocal Tone

The responses to what characteristics help make a good first impression over the telephone are very similar. Whether communicating by telephone or face-to-face interaction, both offer the same challenge and both are difficult to master.

Based on the list of face-to-face characteristics, use the exercise below to compare how they impact your ability to make a good first impression over the telephone.

First Impressions

Check the characteristic you feel helps to make
a good first impression over the telephone:

❑ Responsiveness	❑ Confidence
❑ Demeanor	❑ Rate of Speech
❑ Greeting	❑ Name
❑ Attitude	❑ Eye Contact
❑ Appearance	❑ Informative
❑ Vocal Tone	❑ Posture
❑ Good Listener	❑ Courteousness
❑ Handshake	❑ Pleasantness
❑ Body Language	❑ Recall Ability
❑ Articulate	❑ Friendliness
❑ Smile	❑ Attentiveness
❑ Sincerity	❑ Helpfulness

How many characteristics did you select? _____

Any surprises? Are you amazed that nearly all face-to-face characteristics are transferable to basic telephone communication? They're transferable because the majority of these characteristics are related to your attitude.

Remember, if communicating over the telephone, your customers can't see your smile or how well-dressed you are. They can't make eye contact with you or exchange a nice, firm handshake. So if you want to make a good first impression over the telephone, you must learn to display these characteristics in your voice.

Which of the above characteristics would help you improve your telephone communication skills?

1. _____

2. _____

3. _____

4. _____

5. _____

Make certain these characteristics can be heard in your voice.

This foreword gives you an overview of the practical applications you'll find throughout **Beyond "Hello".** Each chapter is filled with useful tips, tools, exercises and examples you can use to improve your telephone skills and personality. But remember, it all starts with your attitude.

Chapter 1

"Our attitude is the crayon that colors our world."
– Allen Klein

Attitude:
Now You Hear It–Now You Don't

What is attitude? The most talked about attitude, of course, is the infamous negative or "bad" attitude. Ask people if they have an attitude and you're insinuating that their disposition is sour, grumpy or discouraging. Their manner of speaking may be abrupt, rude or forceful and their approach to any given situation might be negative, self-serving or inconsiderate. No one wants to interact with someone who displays negativity.

When asked why you enjoy working with your favorite customers, you'll likely identify their positive attitude as the major reason. You see them as having great perspective and pleasant temperament. They're high spirited and exhibit sensitivity in most situations. We enjoy relationships with people whose positive attitudes enrich our lives. It's comforting and enjoyable when our customers, coworkers, managers or supervisors demonstrate a positive attitude.

Your attitude impacts the level of customer service you provide. It even impacts your ability to successfully sell your product or service. It's imperative you treat customers with respect and give them more than they expect. Make their experience of dealing with your company as pleasant as possible.

Most people exhibit a good attitude toward customers. Everyone experiences bad days—times when you're not at your best. It's impossible to always be positive, but you can certainly temper your negative feelings when they occur. It's easy to forget how productivity and customer relationships suffer because of a negative attitude.

Have you ever taken a negative attitude to work? If the workday progresses without a hitch, chances are your attitude will improve. But, if your day is riddled with irate callers, tight deadlines, too many meetings, conflict or delays, it's likely you'll have a worse attitude than the one you had.

How does your attitude impact the level of customer service you provide? How does it impact a potential sale? What impact does your attitude have on your productivity throughout the workday?

The answers to these questions can be difficult to provide when your expectations are different than those of your customer. Namely, the customer will suffer the consequences of your negative attitude.

Everyone in an organization is a salesperson and the impression, positive or negative, each person makes is an advertisement for the company. This can add up to hundreds or thousands of advertisements delivered each day. So, a company can't risk turning customers off by displaying a negative attitude or indifference to them over the telephone.

You'll have greater success retaining customers when you learn to manage a positive attitude and improve your skills in the following areas.

Put A Smile In Your Voice

It's a fact that people can hear a smile through the telephone. Yet, in an effort to process callers quickly, we might forget about sounding warm, friendly, interested or concerned. Our voice helps us reflect the image we present to our customers and helps them see, hear or feel our attitude at that moment. Why? Because it's the voice that projects warmth or coolness, interest or indifference, concern or frustration, understanding or irritability, patience or anxiety, acceptance or resistance.

When your smile can be heard, chances are you convey the right image—the one your customers expect and appreciate—the one that helps you establish a rapport and build long-term, loyal business relationships.

One workshop participant shared a situation that illustrates the value of a smile. Her customer remarked, "You must really enjoy your work." When she asked her customer what he meant, he responded, "I can hear your smile through the telephone—you sound very pleasant and glad to be working with me. I appreciate that. You've made me feel special."

Can your smile be heard? It's difficult to sound cheerful, upbeat and willing to go the extra mile when your facial expression clearly reflects gloom and doom. It may be time for you to take a look in the mirror.

Check out your smile with this simple procedure:

With telephone receiver in hand (or headset in place), look into a mirror and introduce you to yourself with a frown or grimace on your face. Then, try it again with a smile on your face. Listen carefully to the difference in vocal tone, energy level and attitude. It's much easier to sound cheerful when you look cheerful.

We've all answered the phone with negative attitudes. Perhaps, we're in the middle of completing a large project or have several other calls holding; perhaps, we weren't prepared to take a call. Chances are the smile is absent from our initial greeting—until we discover it's our favorite customer or best friend on the line. Have you noticed how quickly the smile comes into your voice when you answer a call from someone you enjoy. You must treat every call as though it's your best friend or favorite customer on the other end.

Incoming calls are more difficult to manage because you're caught off guard and unprepared when the phone rings. Although responsiveness is an important aspect of customer service, it's easy to view incoming calls as interruptions and interpret them as invasions of privacy.

Here are some tips for putting the smile in your voice on a moment's notice:

Can Your Smile Be Heard?

☺ Put a smile in your voice before you answer the telephone—not after.

☺ Extend a pleasant greeting and make your customers feel welcome.

☺ View every call as a welcomed interruption rather than an invasion of privacy.

☺ Avoid distractions. Give your full attention to the customer.

☺ Immediately make note of the customer's name; don't rely on your memory.

☺ Glance in a mirror so you can see your smile before you answer a call.

Look Good To Yourself

Self-esteem—what you think about yourself—is the driving force behind your attitude. It can be the single most important determinant of mental well-being. It's impossible to perform consistently in a manner that's inconsistent with how we view ourselves. People define themselves through a basic sense of pride, dignity, confidence and self-respect and convey these qualities through their relationships with others.

Look at yourself through the eyes of your customer. What do you see? What do you expect to see? Now listen to yourself through the ears of your customer. What do you hear? What do you expect to hear?

◆ Do you sound knowledgeable, friendly and confident? Are you helpful, interested and concerned? Do you sound trustworthy and sincere?

◆ Are you dressed for success? Personal grooming plays a powerful role in how you're perceived. Do you feel good about your appearance? Sometimes our casual, laid back style of dress equates to a lackadaisical or nonchalant attitude. These qualities come through in your voice. Is that what you want your customer to hear?

◆ Is your workspace organized? Are you able to find the resources you need, when you need them to assist the customer properly? Does your desk reflect that of a person who values the placement of priorities and organization? Remember organization demonstrates discipline. Your customers can sense good organizational skills.

◆ Check your attitude. People sense varying levels of anxiety, discomfort, indecisiveness and insecurity through the sound of your voice. Your ability to represent your organization and yourself in the best possible way is important.

◆ Looking good means more than feeling good inside. It also means looking good on the outside, which lets others know how well you view yourself.

The following exercise assesses your attitude and behavior. Use it to keep your attitude in check.

Building A Positive Attitude

	Always	Usually	Seldom
1. I'm patient and understanding.	____	____	____
2. I demonstrate a sense of humor.	____	____	____
3. I put the customer first.	____	____	____
4. I'm willing to go the extra mile.	____	____	____
5. I'm courteous at all times.	____	____	____
6. I'm sensitive to others' needs.	____	____	____
7. I consider all viewpoints.	____	____	____
8. I'm result-oriented.	____	____	____
9. I treat problems as challenges.	____	____	____
10. I do my best to remain positive.	____	____	____
11. I like others and myself.	____	____	____
12. I enjoy working with people.	____	____	____
Total:	____ +	____ +	____ = ____

Scoring:

Award yourself the following points:

Always = 10   Usually = 6   Seldom = 1

Add the number of points for each column to obtain an overall total.

90 - 100 points   = Your attitude is positive, and you're very productive.

80 - 89 points   = Your attitude is generally, but not consistently, positive.

Below 80 points   = You need to assess your behaviors and make some changes to
                                  become more positive.

Most people agree it's not realistic to achieve a score of 95 to 100. As one client put it,
"To say we're always in the best frame of mind can certainly be challenged from various
viewpoints." So, most people score between 80 to 94 points when they respond
truthfully to these statements. Why? Because realistically, we usually exhibit a positive
attitude and seldom admit it when we don't.

Ensure you aren't demonstrating a false sense of security about your attitude by working
through this exercise again. Doing so will help you achieve a balanced and consistent
work attitude.

Develop A "Can Do" Attitude

It's a challenge to always present the best possible image of ourselves. Developing a
"can do" attitude will enhance your ability to achieve greater success in establishing
positive working relationships. When you transmit a positive attitude, people are
naturally more responsive. People respond positively to positive people.

Consider how easy it is to express negative thoughts while in a conversation. Learn to think about the behavior of all involved in a consistently positive manner. Achieving this objective lay in your ability to understand the value of positive language. When you accept responsibility for your own thoughts and actions, you'll embrace the concept of expressing cooperation in customer relationships.

Positive Thinking

Ever heard the old saying, "We're our own worst enemy?" Sometimes it's more comfortable to think, "I've seen the enemy, and it isn't me!" The next time you let negative thoughts influence your ability to think positively about an adverse situation, think again.

Negative self-talk frequently occurs when we make mistakes, misinterpret work assignments or feel devalued by customers or a coworker. Allow your attitude to impact circumstances rather than allowing circumstances to impact your attitude.

We can always blame others for our feelings of inadequacy. We adopt a posture of negative thinking when things don't go well. Learn to be accountable for your own thoughts and actions—think positive! Sometimes you need to assess your initial reaction, work through negative circumstances and take it upon yourself to turn things around. Ask yourself, "What can I do to help this be a more positive situation?"

Some people are unable to turn negativity into a positive mindset. You can create a neutral zone that will carry you into a more positive frame of mind. Reinforce your positive attitude and rid yourself of negative thoughts by using "I" statements. How can "I" turn the following statements into positive thoughts?

Practice Positive Self-Talk

Negative: I hate cleaning up other people's messes!

Positive: _____

_____

Negative: Don't they know these expectations are unrealistic?

Positive: _____

_____

Negative: Forget about good customer service! I'm too angry.

Positive: _____

_____

Negative: No one cares how I feel.

Positive: _____

_____

The purpose of this exercise is to help move you from a strong negative position to one where you can think and respond more positively. Each response should incorporate an "I" statement that demonstrates your ability to understand the impact positive thinking has on negative thoughts. For most of us, it's not easy to consistently incorporate positive thoughts. Make a habit of replacing negative, helpless thoughts with positive, powerful ones. Turn negative self-talk into positive-self-talk. Rephrasing negative statements into positive statements works for all areas of your life.

Positive Language

Research has shown that people understand and respond one-third more quickly to positive words than negative ones. Consider how you react when people use negative language in conversation with you. Notice how you respond differently when specific comments or requests are phrased in a more positive manner.

Once you overcome negative self-talk, speaking in positives will occur naturally. Make a conscious effort to communicate with your customers using positive words that solicit the response you desire. The following words and phrases typically elicit a negative response from customers.

"I'll try"

Feedback from our clients indicates that when you say "I'll try" it really means: "Maybe I'll do it; maybe I won't," "I'll patronize you; I'll make you think we can pull this off," or "I'll say whatever sounds good to you." Except in the instances where you know the person well, the customer sounds really sincere, or you believe everyone means what they say, "I'll try," means nothing.

In general, you know if a task can be done. If it can't be done, just say so. If you're uncertain, let the customer know you'll "make every effort to see that it's done" and "do your best to make it happen," that you'll "give it your best shot" or, at the least, "see what you can do."

Imagine ordering dinner in your favorite restaurant and the waiter telling you he'll "try" to place your order. Of course, this is unacceptable. At the very least, you expect him to place your order and, if he doesn't place your order, you certainly deserve an explanation as to why he was unable to do so.

"You'll have to"

People don't like being made to feel as though they have to do anything—least of all, business with you. However, your customers may need to follow certain procedures so your internal processes flow smoothly. Polite requests for action, "May I ask you to?" or "Will you please?" or "I would appreciate your..." accompanied by a brief explanation are much better alternatives to, "You'll have to...." Remember to put the smile in your voice when you make a request of customers. You'll sound friendlier and much less demanding. Think about how you feel when someone from another company tells you what you have to do. Are you offended by their dictatorial attitude? Do you often wonder why it needs to be done? Or, are you more willing to comply when the request is friendly and less demanding?

Imagine the local video store salesperson says, "You have to complete our credit application in order to rent videos from our store." Well, you don't care to divulge credit information just to rent videos. Your response will most likely be negative. Why? Because you know there are other video stores in your neighborhood that don't require the completion of a credit application. You respond, "Thanks-but-no-thanks. I'll take my business elsewhere," reminding the company and yourself that you don't have to do anything you don't want to do.

In today's competitive environment, you have many alternatives for choosing where you do business. Most important, so do your customers.

"I'll be honest with you"

Integrity is the foundation upon which relationships are built, strengthened and nurtured. Customers expect honesty and sincerity in business dealings. Honesty builds long-term loyalty and trust in relationships. Everyone likes to believe people are sincere when they say, "I'll be honest with you." How do you feel when someone says, "I'll be honest with you?" If you have a relationship with that individual, you'll accept the word "honest." If you don't have an established relationship, you may be skeptical.

The average person interprets this phrase as an invitation to accept a forthcoming lie. That is, they don't expect to hear the truth. Unfortunately, honest doesn't have the same meaning as it once did. However, it does still mean "truthful." This is what your customers expect from you. They expect you'll at least be truthful. Use phrases like "the truth is" or "truthfully speaking" to gain your customer's trust.

Brian, an attendee at our training seminar, summed it up: "I'll be honest with you is like saying, *no offense, but I'm going to offend you now."*

Barbara, another participant, explained how she impatiently awaits the surprise following a declaration of honesty. She says, "I know there's more to come. Is it going to be good or bad news? Do I need to sit down?"

"I don't know"

Your customers expect you to be knowledgeable about the operation of your organization or respective department and about the products and services you provide. If you don't know the answer, ask someone who does. Let the customer know "That's a good question. Let me find out for you," or "I am eager to understand that better myself. I will let you know what I learn."

There's nothing wrong with not knowing everything. Your responsibility is to search for the answer and make note of the appropriate response for future reference. Be sure to follow up with the customer and provide status updates, if necessary. Share the information with other coworkers so they'll be informed as well.

"I can't"

Remember that success comes in "cans." Rather than letting your customer know you "can't" have the technician at their location until Friday, let them know you "can" or "will" have the technician there on Friday.

Your positive response and display of confidence will reinforce your commitment toward customer satisfaction. If you're confident the task can't be done, consider substituting the word "can't" with the phrase "I'm sorry, I'm unable to...."

Create Mutual Reliance

Don't bite the hand that feeds you! Mutual reliance is one of the many keys to successful business relationships. Your primary objective is to satisfy customer needs. Positive thinking—first to yourself and second about your customer response—gives you a greater opportunity to strengthen relationships.

Take ownership of your ability to establish a value-added alliance with the customer. After all, you're a public relations representative for your company. You represent the partnership your company wants to have with its customers. You're an integral part of the customer's perception of your organization.

Don't play a self-serving role. Most people think of "XYZ Company" as you: the person they deal with on a regular basis; the person they depend on for a long-term, healthy relationship; the person who makes them feel special. Practice weaving your customer into the fabric of your organization by speaking in a manner that expresses mutual respect and conveys a message that they're part of your company.

Think about a recent conversation you've had with a customer. How many times did you use the word "I"? How often did you use language that made them feel like one of your team? The following examples of mutual reliance demonstrate interest and concern for all involved.

<u>**Self-Serving**</u>	<u>**Mutual Reliance**</u>
I value your business	We value your business
My point is	Our position is
I'm on your side	We aim to please
I don't understand	Let's clarify our objectives
I don't see it that way	We can work it out

Mutual reliance invisibly shapes perception and can turn debate into dialog and vice versa. Use these substitutions for effective customer communication:

Instead of *critique* use *comment*
Instead of *other side* use *another side*
Instead of *having an argument* use *making an argument*
Instead of *focus on differences* use *search for common ground*

Friendly Reminders:

➢ What you do demonstrates your behavior.

➢ Exhibit a balanced and consistent attitude.

➢ How you feel demonstrates your attitude.

➢ Sound knowledgeable, friendly and confident.

➢ Dress for success. Feel good about your appearance.

➢ Maintain an organized workspace.

➢ Disorganization can be heard over the telephone.

➢ Put a smile in your voice.

➢ Look good to yourself.

➢ Develop a "can do" attitude.

➢ Create mutual reliance.

Chapter 2

"You cannot shake hands with a clenched fist."
– Indira Gandhi

How To Say "Hello":
Guidelines For Professional Greetings

As with initial introductions in face-to-face encounters, your telephone greeting helps you present a memorable image, makes the customer feel welcome and builds a rapport in support of your organization's customer service goals. How's your greeting? Are you making callers feel welcome?

Some people consistently perform well on the telephone. They enjoy working with customers and find telephone work challenging; they have a smile in their voice with every greeting which exhibits a positive attitude; they're pleasant, helpful and confident; they transmit enthusiasm when accepting or placing calls.

When you work in a repetitive environment, however, many aspects of customer interaction may become robotic. You may sound dull, boring or monotonous. You may lack enthusiasm, interest or concern, yet expect the customer to understand.

Most important, is how you deliver your telephone greeting. This is where first impressions begin. Many telephone greetings are lengthy which causes an anxious caller to interrupt mid-sentence before your greeting is complete, for example:

Thank you for calling Green Tree Trimming Services, caretakers of the foliage that beautifies your home. We offer full indoor and outdoor service to care for your plants and trees as if they were in our own front yards! This is Robert, how may I help you?

On the other hand, some greetings are too short and don't provide enough information for the caller. These greetings may come across as abrupt or rude, for example:

This is Traci.

A greeting should not exceed 10 seconds. Customize your greeting by thinking about how each word in your greeting will impact overall delivery. Then determine which elements of your greeting are most appropriate.

Offer A Salutation

A salutation on the telephone is similar to a handshake. It's a favorable way to say "welcome" or "hello."

Since most calls these days are answered by voice messaging systems, we seldom expect to hear a "live" person on the other end of the telephone line. Many times we're unprepared to speak when we do receive a "live" response. Have you ever answered a call, delivered your greeting, and received no response? You wait a second. You say "hello?" to the silence then discover someone on the line. The most common response from the caller is "Oh, I'm sorry. I was expecting to get voice mail" or "You sounded like a voice mail recording, I was waiting for the beep."

Opening your greeting with a salutation helps callers know they have made contact with a "live" person. It enables them to quickly collect their thoughts and respond in a timely manner. A friendly "good morning" or "good afternoon" is the best place to begin.

Remember to glance in the mirror and check your attitude before you answer each call; you must also be aware of the time of day. Be accurate when you say "good morning" or "good afternoon." Have you ever answered the phone at 1:10 p.m. by saying "good morning...?" Situations like this can be embarrassing and send mixed messages to the caller. This usually occurs when you function in robotic mode or simply aren't concentrating on the call.

"Thank you for calling　" is a great alternative salutation. Perhaps, you answer calls from a toll-free telephone number or deal with customers in international time zones. For instance, the corporate call center for one of our major clients operates 24 hours a day, seven days a week. Call receipt agents accept calls from around the world. In this scenario, "Thank you for calling..." is the most appropriate salutation.

State Your Company Name

It's important to identify your company by name, particularly when you're the first point of contact and are responsible for routing calls to appropriate destinations. Your customers want to know they've reached the right place.

Some company names are lengthy, making it difficult to easily say. Be mindful of pronunciation and enunciation. Slow the rate of your speech and pause slightly to distinguish one word from another. When words run together, you come across as mumbled or muffled, which comes across as inarticulate and garbled. Law firms are a good example as many have four or more partners included in the corporate name. For example: Marx, Thomas, Schinqler, Henderson and Zipoweitz, Attorneys at Law.

When writing the name of the company, we can easily use Marx, Thomas et al.—meaning, "and others." On the telephone, partners expect their name to be included in the greeting. There is seldom an opportunity to abbreviate without hurting someone's feelings. In some companies, it's understood that the names of all partners are incorporated under the umbrella of the corporation, e.g., The Schinqler Group.

Some companies creatively offer an advertising message as part of their corporate greeting. One of our clients is known as a national personal development organization. They have developed an outstanding reputation for conveying their message of "positive thinking for positive results" to customers through books, tapes and other learning material, and they want everyone to know it. The company's standard telephone greeting sounds like this:

ThankyouforcallingCareerEnhancementAssociates,authorsofthe
positivethinkingforpositiveresultsphilosophy...

Can you decipher this greeting? Make your delivery more effective by slowing your rate of speech, pausing between phrases or words and articulating each word. This helps the listener understand what's being said, for example:

Thank you for calling Career Enhancement Associates, (pause)
authors of the positive thinking (pause) for positive results philosophy...

Some companies and organizations are better known by acronyms, e.g., ACME, NHT, CONOCO. It's easy to slip into robotic mode when pronouncing acronyms. Don't be caught off guard—always enunciate clearly and carefully.

State Your Department Name

When answering a call within your department or accepting calls on your direct-dial line, be sure to state the name of your department. To say, "This is Marsha" is unacceptable. Make a conscious effort to identify your department. The best examples I've heard include:

You've reached Marsha Scott in the
Accounting Department of Web Design International.
or
Thank you for calling the customer support group of Select Properties International.

Many calls are misdirected. Your customers will appreciate knowing they've been connected with the appropriate department.

Give Your Name

Using your name in the greeting gives the caller a point of reference for future interaction with your company. It also gives you an opportunity to establish a rapport with the caller.

Repeating our name on the phone numerous times throughout the workday often causes us to forget how names impact customer relationships. State your name clearly. Speak at a pace that is easy to understand and carefully pronounce your name so the caller can repeat it. Be especially sensitive to the caller's need for clarity when your name is difficult to pronounce.

Whether or not you use both first and last name is your choice. In most cases, identifying yourself by first and last name is an excellent marketing tool, particularly in sales and other professional environments.

Imagine a potential customer attending a local chamber of commerce business after-hours event. The prospect engages in a conversation with one of your newest clients who speak highly of your company's product or service and the great relationship he or she has with you. The prospect asks for your name so he or she can contact you for future business and your customer says: "His name is Charles. He works at XYZ Company. I don't know his last name. Just call the main number and ask to speak with Charles in the mutual funds department. They'll know who he is."

Did you miss a sales opportunity? Wouldn't it be better for your customer to say: "I work with Charles Melvin in the mutual funds department at XYZ Company. Call him. I know you won't be disappointed with his performance."

Many companies employ people with identical first names and sometimes with identical last names. Take advantage of the opportunity to distinguish yourself from the others by using your last name. Once you begin identifying yourself by first and last name, callers will ask for you that way. Think about how quickly you can process a call when you don't need to ask, "Which Connie do you want to speak with?" or "Do you know Tony's last name?"

Some companies and organizations don't want employees to use their last name when working with customers or clients on the telephone. Keep in mind that in some work environments, last name usage isn't permissible because of the specific nature of the business, e.g., abuse shelters, call centers, help lines, etc.

Offer Assistance

To serve customers well, you must be knowledgeable about your products and services. In most instances, you also need to be knowledgeable about various workgroup activities and departmental operations.

Do you offer assistance to callers when the person being contacted is unavailable to accept the call? Are you helpful? Do you know others in your organization or workgroup who can help meet the customer's need?

How do you offer assistance at the close of your greeting? What you say will impact the outcome of the call. Why? Because there is a significant difference between: "How may I help you?" and "How may I direct your call?"

The following interpretations will help you create the appropriate greeting closure for your situation.

"How may I help you?"

When you give a customer the impression you're the person who can help them, they assume you're the appropriate person to talk with about their reason for calling. As a result, people might spend 35 to 60 seconds explaining their need to the wrong person.

Have you ever received a call from a customer who gives intricate details about their reason for calling? Sometimes you don't need all of the facts. You need only enough information or detail to route the call to the appropriate person or department. In most instances, you know halfway through the call that the person should be connected with someone else. Yet, you patiently—or impatiently—listen and then say, "I'll transfer you to...."

When you're the recipient of the transferred call, you might wonder why callers sound a bit annoyed when you ask, "How may I help you?" It's usually because they need to repeat the details of their reason for calling. Perhaps, the caller misinterpreted the manner in which you offered assistance. This greeting is helpful only for those who can address the caller's need immediately.

I once returned a call to a client whose executive assistant found a creative yet professional way to greet callers on his behalf. Her greeting is upbeat and she does a great job of keeping the smile in her voice as she says, "This is Mena, XYZ Company, answering for Butch Wright. How may I help you?"

"How may I direct your call?"

When customers hear this offer of assistance, they usually assume you're responsible for connecting them with an appropriate person or department who can address their need. Most callers know they might need to share some information with you regarding their reason for calling and are more than willing to do so. They assume they'll be transferred to someone who can help. In most instances, the caller will provide a brief summary of facts, versus a lengthy explanation. In any case, they'd prefer not to repeat the information to the person who receives the call following the transfer.

This greeting is most helpful for front office support personnel and those who manage calls for several people within a workgroup or department.

Just help!

In the spirit of teamwork... just help! Do whatever is necessary to provide immediate assistance for the caller. If Magdalene is on vacation, put the caller in touch with the person who has taken over her responsibilities. If Dennis is in a meeting or at lunch, connect the caller with someone who can provide immediate assistance. If you provide direct administrative support for the person being contacted, consider what you can do to help. Can you connect this caller with another department, take a message, offer voice mail, answer the question yourself or call back with an appropriate response?

Several months ago, I returned a long distance phone call to a potential customer in Minneapolis. I remember the experience quite well and probably will for a long time. Here's what happened:

A young man answered the phone. He had a smile in his voice and sounded friendly. He didn't give the impression of being rushed or hurried, and he was polite.

Young man: *Good morning. XYZ Company.*

Jeannie: *Good morning. This is Jeannie Davis in Denver. I'm returning a call to Ms. Kane.*

Young man: *She's not here Ma'am.*

Jeannie: *Oh, will she be in the office this afternoon?*

Young man: *I don't know Ma'am.*

Jeannie: *Does she have voice mail? Perhaps, I can leave a message.*

Young man: *No Ma'am.*

Jeannie: *Silence. (I'm waiting for his offer of assistance).*

Young man: *Silence*

Jeannie: *I'm returning her call. How best would you suggest I get a message to her?*

Young man: *I don't know Ma'am. She had a funeral.*

Jeannie: *Thank you.*

What's wrong with this picture? As friendly and polite as this young man sounded, he didn't offer to help me, nor did he volunteer to take a message. He also didn't tell me his name. He couldn't tell me when the woman would return—if ever—as it occurred to me the funeral she was attending could be her own! I was reluctant to ask who the "dearly departed" was as I didn't think it was my business. Of course, I could have insisted he take a message, but then I wouldn't have this shining example to share with you! Besides, would you trust this guy to properly record your message and get it to the right person? I don't think so!

Guideline for Professional Greetings

A professional telephone greeting includes at least three of these ingredients:

Salutation
Good Morning
Good Afternoon
Thank you for calling

Company Name

Department Name

Your Name

An Offer of Assistance—Select from the following:
How may I help you?
How may I direct your call?

Just Help!

People will form an opinion of you within 15 seconds based on your greeting and response. Give careful consideration to the elements contained in your greeting. Remember to be pleasant, keep the smile in your voice and demonstrate your willingness to help.

Friendly Reminders:

➤ Create a positive first impression through your confidence, attitude, appearance and smile.

➤ Offset the possibility of sounding robotic by using the Guideline for Professional Greetings as a menu for creating various greetings throughout the year.

➤ Change your greeting periodically so you don't sound boring or monotonous.

➤ Slow your rate of speech when delivering a lengthy greeting. Enunciate words and pause where appropriate.

Chapter 3

"The answer is contained within the question."
– Ancient Proverb

Call Screening And Probing:
Getting The Information You Need

Make every effort to be helpful and courteous when screening calls and probing for information. Demonstrate interest and concern for the caller's need or request. Your challenge is to make one customer feel as important as any other. Learn to screen calls in a professional manner; and although you may be the designated gatekeeper, avoid turning probing into an inquisition.

Call-Screening Options

Remember, people want to feel special as though their reason for calling is valid. Sometimes we don't manage the call-screening process well because we simply don't know how. We believe asking the traditional "polite" questions are the only way to obtain appropriate information. Often, we're told exactly what to say without regard for the sensitivity of the caller. Mostly, we forget to treat people the way we expect to be treated. We stand a good chance of losing business for our company when we come across as nosey, bossy, demanding or indifferent when screening calls.

How do you feel when someone answers your call, asks for your name, asks what your call is regarding and immediately puts you on hold? How do you feel when they then return only to let you know the person you want to speak with is busy, in a meeting, not available at the moment or has stepped away from his or her desk?

Undoubtedly, you feel insignificant or discounted when calls are screened in this manner. Your call-screening techniques must prevent this. Take the initiative and develop an acceptable call-screening technique with the person in charge. Working together, you'll avoid some of the experiences that hamper the effectiveness of others. Here are a few of their stories:

An executive assistant in one company feels his credibility is at stake because client calls aren't returned. He reports:

I'm always frustrated with my boss when it comes to screening calls. I screen every call at his request. He never answers his phone personally, doesn't mind people being dumped into voice mail and seldom returns calls in a timely manner, if at all. His behavior causes people to repeatedly call back. I'm the one who listens to their disappointment, concern and frustration about not hearing from him. Sometimes people question whether I delivered the message and, if I did, why he hasn't returned the call.

Dorothy is a customer service representative who vows to never again work for someone who asks her to lie. She says:

My boss never wants to talk to salespeople. Sales calls aren't allowed to get through to her and if one inadvertently does, I've got hell to pay as a result! I've asked for permission to tell these people she's not interested, but she prefers I say she's not here. I feel so badly for them. My brothers are salesmen and I think they have a right to make a living. Maybe you can help, Jeannie. What can I do?

A colleague in the National Speaker's Association shared this experience:

A potential customer asked that I contact her in 30 days. I pride myself on being timely; I think it helps convey a sense of responsibility and professionalism. When I made contact, the administrative assistant used the "hand-over-mouthpiece" technique to let Ms. Jones know I was on the line. I overheard her say, "He's a pain in the neck. There's no need for me to talk to him. Tell him whatever you want. Eventually, he'll stop calling." I was furious and I let them both know it!

I returned a call to a person who had requested information about our training programs. During the screening process, I responded politely to all questions. Here's how the call was handled:

When I told the person I was with Now Hear This, Inc., she asked, "What do you do?" I appreciated her curiosity and replied accordingly. She informed me "the company has an in-house training department and I don't think your services are needed." I repeated what was said in my initial greeting: "I'm returning her call; let me speak with her, please."

Although I'm known to offer expert advice on telephone communication, I'm cautious not to overstep the boundaries of employer/employee relationships. How would you respond to the workshop participant who commented:

If the boss doesn't have the guts to say "no" or tell the caller "I'm not interested," something is wrong. Why do they have us do their dirty work for them? It makes me look bad and I don't appreciate it.

There are many scenarios for call screening—most are polite, some are unacceptable, others are ineffective, some are interrogatory and few are professional. Here are some call-screening techniques you should consider.

Taboo Screen

Over the years, I've compiled a list of how my calls have been screened. Each example sends the message that some of us need to enhance our skills in this area. Do any of these questions sound familiar?

> *Who's calling?"*
> *What's your name?*
> *Will she know who you are?*
> *What's it regarding?*
> *Will he know what it's about?*
> *Which company are you with?*
> *What's the name of your company?*
> *What's the nature of your business?*
> *What do you do?*
> *Are you a salesperson?*
> *Are you selling something?*

This direct line of questioning can appear to be rude, abrupt or insensitive. These questions are taboo. Don't make your customers feel as though they're on the firing line!

Traditional Screen

Most of us are polite and courteous when call screening is required. Many of us have encountered the impolite caller who, at some point in time, has been advised not to give you too much information. The traditional method of screening calls is sometimes ineffective. Why? Because when you ask permission to do something, people can grant your request or deny it. You give them the opportunity to say no when you ask:

> *May I tell her who is calling, please?*
> *May I ask what your call is in regard to?*
> *May I have your phone number, please?*
> *May I have him return your call?*

Sounds professional enough, right? Think "yes" or "no" as you read each question again. Have you ever been told "no" in response to your attempt to obtain information? Sometimes people refuse to leave their name or reply, "It's personal" or "No thanks, I'll call back later."

This traditional call-screening technique may not produce the desired outcome. What else can you do?

Indirect Screen

Do you really have to ask permission when you need to obtain pertinent information? In most situations, an indirect line of questioning enables you to obtain relevant information without sounding permissive. This call-screening technique also demonstrates your interest and concern for the caller. It says, *I am glad you've called and will do whatever I can to help, so (you must) "let me" have the information I need to serve you properly.* It makes you appear to be a willing participant in the information exchange.

Notice if the customer responds in a friendlier manner when you say:

> *Let me tell Gloria who is calling.*
> *Let me tell Mr. Morton the reason for your call.*
> *Let me take your number so Tami can return your call.*
> *Let me tell Rick what company you're with.*

Using the indirect question technique for call screening increases the likelihood you'll obtain the desired information. Keep in mind that your customer can get around answering any question.

Fill-In-The-Blank Screen

Using the fill-in-the-blank technique indirectly asks your customer to "tell me more...." When you deliver your greeting professionally, there's a smile in your voice and you demonstrate interest and concern for the caller. You have a great opportunity to establish a rapport by saying:

> *And your name is...*
> *And your call is regarding...*
> *And you are with...*
> *And the name of your company is...*
> *And your phone number is...*

This call-screening technique allows you to interact with the customer in an interesting way, without the intimidation of asking direct questions.

Probing Types

Sometimes we need to ask relevant, productive questions to determine how best to serve our customer. When you know your product or service well and keep abreast of departmental operations, you're in a better position to probe.

To "probe" means to feel out, to explore, to investigate, to discover and to question. There are two techniques found to be most helpful in acquiring information. Enhance your probing skills by asking open- or closed-end questions. Knowing the difference between the two will help you probe effectively, not offensively.

Open-End Probes

Many times customers may have difficulty explaining their specific need. Some customers describe their situation and aren't certain what their need is or how best you can help. Others are simply uncommunicative and need a little probing in order for you to understand their need.

Open-end probes encourage people to talk freely and expand on a particular area of discussion. When you want more information, ask open-end questions.

Let's explore two scenarios using the open-end probe technique.

Scenario #1   You're a salesperson for a local newspaper probing to get information that will help build a sales strategy to obtain the customer's order.

You ask: *What details are important to you about newspaper advertisement?*

From a sales perspective, this open-end probe will encourage the customer to tell you more. You have a greater opportunity to learn about the customer's primary advertising concerns as well as their likes and dislikes. Asking this question allows the prospect to provide specific information for building your sales strategy.

Using an open-end probe technique can help you be more creative when describing the benefits and features your newspaper has to offer in order to create an ad that specifically meets customer requirements.

Scenario #2   You're a customer service representative for a local newspaper probing to identify reasons why the customer is dissatisfied with a recent advertisement.

You ask: *What expectations weren't met in your newspaper advertisement?*

From a customer service perspective, this open-end probe invites the customer to tell you why the ad did not meet their expectations. Perhaps, relevant details of their initial request were not communicated clearly or were misunderstood. Open-end probing can provide the means for you to understand why the customer is dissatisfied with his or her current ad.

Use this technique as an opportunity to listen, learn and eventually provide feedback to the design team so appropriate changes can be made.

Can you think of other open-end probes that would be useful in this situation?

Example: How would you describe the ideal advertisement for your company?

1. _____

2. _____

3. _____

Closed-End Probes

There are situations that require probing questions in order to draw closure, to verify information and to obtain agreement so you can proceed. It's important you and your customer have a clear understanding of expectations and outcomes.

Closed-end probes typically restrict the customer's response and are usually answered by "yes," "no," or a limited choice of alternatives.

Let's explore two scenarios using an identical closed-end probe.

You ask: *Don't you agree this will enhance the value of your company's advertisement?*

Scenario #1   From a sales perspective, your objective is to verify information in order to obtain agreement about your product or service proposal. Knowing you've reached agreement gives you approval to move forward with closing the sale.

Scenario #2   From a customer service perspective, you're confirming satisfaction. Asking a closed-end question can assure that the customer's expectations have been met. You have an opportunity to let the customer know you hear their concern and will work diligently to implement the requested changes.

Can you think of other closed-end probes that would be useful in this situation?

Example: Do these solutions adequately address your concerns?

1. _____

2. _____

3. _____

Combination Probe

Developing your probing skills is a great way to up-sell your company's products and services. Many of our clients are expected to "sell without selling." Using a combination of open- and closed-end probes enables you to gather pertinent information and offer appropriate alternatives, for example:

Customer: *Do you have an advertising section for lawn equipment?*

You: *Not at this time. Our advertising campaign for lawn equipment begins in March.*

Customer: *Oh, I see.*

You: *Are you currently offering special pricing on lawn and garden*
(closed)   *equipment?*

Customer: *Yes. As a matter of fact, we want to get a head start on the competition.*

You: *What type of advertisement do you have in mind?*
(open)

Can you think of other combination probes that would be useful in this situation?
For example:

You: *Do you need to run an advertisement for summer lawn care now?*
(closed)

Customer: *Yes. As a matter of fact, we want to get a head start on the competition.*

You: *How can we help your company accomplish that objective before the*
(open)   *spring campaign begins?*

Closed-End Probe

1._____

2._____

3._____

Open-End Probe

1._____

2._____

3._____

Practice using these techniques to obtain necessary information from your customer. Your challenge: To listen carefully to the customer's response.

Friendly Reminders:

➤ Make it a point to discuss call-screening preferences with the person(s) in charge. Work together to create a comfortable environment for all involved.

➤ Calls are screened to obtain pertinent information, e.g., name, number and reason for calling.

➤ Answer the pre-screened call with a personable greeting.

➤ When you've already screened the call and find the person being contacted is unavailable or simply doesn't want to be disturbed, you might say: "Let me take your name and phone number so he/she can return your call."

➤ Avoid screening a call by covering the telephone receiver with your hand—press the hold button!

➤ Remember that voice mail isn't the only alternative. Offer assistance!

➤ Don't abuse your telephone power! You have the ability to make or break a business relationship.

➤ Ask probing questions from a position of curiosity. This demonstrates your genuine interest and concern for seeking the information required.

➤ When asking for specific information, begin your questions with "what," "who" or "when."

➤ When seeking clarity of information, begin your questions with "how" or "where."

➤ When soliciting general information to gain a better understanding of the entire situation, begin your questions with "Could you tell me more about...?"

➤ Questions that seek closure or agreement generally begin with *do, did, is, will* or *don't you agree.*

➤ Avoid asking questions that begin with "why." In most instances, "why" questions trigger a defensive response that typically begins with "Because...."

➤ Be mindful that vocal tone can impact the response to every question you ask. Don't sound condescending.

Chapter 4

"Patience is never more important than when you're on the verge of losing it."

– Anonymous

Call Transfer And Holding: Handling Calls Like A Pro

Give special care to the manner in which you transfer callers or place them on hold. Have you been put on hold for an excessive amount of time or transferred to various departments before finally reaching the appropriate destination? Keep in mind that first impressions perceived by first-time callers become lasting memories. You play a key role in creating whatever image the customer perceives when the introductory call takes place. Remember that each customer interaction is an advertisement for you and the company.

Transferring Calls

What feelings do you experience upon hearing that your call must be transferred? Most often, the phrase "I'll transfer your call..." is perceived as a negative experience. Even though it's necessary, the caller frequently feels discounted or unimportant. Often the way the transition is handled leaves a lot to be desired. Any telephone call can be misdirected, unanswered, picked up by voice mail or bounced back to its original station.

This makes the call transfer crucial to the customer-company relationship. Imagine you're introducing the customer to people within various departments of your company. How will you effectively manage the transition of each telephone call from one person to another?

What we feel when our call is transferred isn't surprising. Customers seem to have little or no patience when being transferred several times; they simply don't want to bounce from department to department. Here's a sampling of how customers feel when they hear the word "transfer":

> *Here we go again!*
> *I suppose it's necessary, but I hate it.*
> *I wonder where I'll end up this time.*
> *Why can't they get it right the first time?*
> *I feel like I'm getting the run-around!*
> *Is everyone too busy to care why I'm calling?*

Even when the reason for the transfer is valid, we may experience an inappropriate transfer or end up dumped on the doorstep of an unsuspecting company representative. Therefore, it's imperative that you learn to manage call transfers smoothly, efficiently and courteously. You can minimize the frustration for all involved by following these tips for making the right connections.

Don't "Transfer" the Call

Make every effort not to activate a customer's defense mechanism. What you really want to do is connect the person with someone in your organization who can help. Instead of the word "transfer," use alternative words and phrases that sound more positive to the customer.

Here are some suggested alternatives:

> *I'll connect you with Jason now.*
> *I'll send your call to our Editorial Department.*
> *I'll have Ava in our customer support group handle your call.*
> *I'll forward your call to Joyce; she can help you.*
> *I'll put you in touch with our Payroll Department.*

There are several other alternatives that may fit your company's circumstances. Brainstorm with the person in charge and challenge your workgroup to find creative ways to make the right connection.

Dead-End Transfer

Avoid delivering a dead-end transfer. Treat the customer as though you welcome the call and are proud to introduce them to someone in your company. A dead-end transfer occurs when you send the caller to another person or department and immediately hang up without knowing if the call connected. The customer has been dumped, so to speak.

Make a conscious effort to personally escort customers to their destination. Remain on the line with the caller until the call connects or until you're certain the call gets to the appropriate person or department. Introduce the customer and provide a brief description of their reason for calling. Most telephone systems provide a perfect opportunity to introduce the caller before transferring the call. You might say:

> *Leon, Mr. Patterson is on the line with us. He's calling about a discrepancy in his bank account.*

> *Mr. Merick, I am forwarding a call from Sean Farr regarding quality control. I'll connect you now, Mr. Farr.*

> *Clyde, your call has been connected with LaToya Dunn in customer service. Have a great day!*

Delores, Ms. Rucker has been holding for sometime. She needs help understanding our new billing procedures. Thank you for calling, Ms. Rucker.

Utilizing this call transfer technique gives you another opportunity to provide great customer service. By staying on the line, you'll be there to help when the person called is unavailable, there's no answer, voice mail responds or the line is busy. You're in a better position to offer immediate assistance, take a message, route the call to someone else or ask whether the customer prefers to leave a voice mail message.

Dead-end transfers are unavoidable in some organizations, for example: you work for a large bank and have tried staying on the line with customers, but your call volume is unusually heavy and there's no time to wait with the customer until someone picks up the line. You might say:

I'll connect you with the Accounting Department.
Someone will be with you momentarily.

Provide Information—Be Helpful!

Your customers don't like being dumped! They prefer to know where they're going and why. When you're unable to stay with the call until a connection has been made, become an information provider. Demonstrate your interest and concern for making the right connection by giving the customer relevant information in the event the call is inadvertently disconnected, for example:

Let me give you Buddy's direct-dial phone number in case we're disconnected.

I'll forward your call to LaShawn in our Tax Department; her extension is 146.

Dr. Varma is available for consultation between 3 and 4 p.m. on Monday and Wednesday. Her telephone number is...

Whenever possible, give the caller the following information before transferring the call:

◆ Name of person
◆ Name of department
◆ Telephone number
◆ Telephone extension
◆ Hours of availability or operation

Now you've serviced the customer by providing information. If there's a disconnection, the customer can call back and ask for that person by name or re-dial the telephone number directly. Using this call transfer technique also gives the customer a chance to make note of contact information for future reference.

Be Knowledgeable

Do you know who does what in your organization or workgroup? Make every effort to learn more about departmental work activities and day-to-day operations of your company. Utilize every resource available for determining appropriate distribution channels for telephone calls.

Start thinking about corporate resources that provide contact information necessary for you to do your job well. Helpful resources might include:

◆ Organization chart
◆ Employee directory
◆ Department directory
◆ Procedure manuals
◆ List of key contact person names
◆ Quick reference guides
◆ List of emergency procedures
◆ Emergency telephone numbers
◆ List of internal "hotline" numbers
◆ List of employee resource organizations

Don't be caught unprepared. Make certain you have easy access to all available information resources. Remember to make note of the appropriate contact person or department so you won't have to ask for the information over and over again.

Hold The Line

In our workshop, many of the questions about putting customers on hold relate to the problem of having to do many tasks at once. Perhaps, there are several other people on hold, someone standing nearby demanding your immediate attention, meanwhile you're listening to a customer's life history, and you're in the middle of a large project—so you forget who's holding for whom. Your frustration may come through in your voice. What happened to your smile, looking good to yourself and your positive "can-do" attitude?

Unfortunately, you'll need to place callers on hold. But keep in mind that to hold means to control, imprison, clench, grip, clutch, grasp. The only thing that helps convey a friendlier, more professional approach to placing customers on hold is your willingness to understand their frustration with that process. You can smoothly meet the challenge of placing customers on hold and minimize frustration for all involved by following these guidelines.

First Things First

It's important that you're prepared to take the call. Here are some tips that will help you treat each call as though it was the first one of the day.

❑ Take a deep breath.

It might sound silly to suggest you take a deep breath before answering the call, especially when you're rushed or hurried, but it really does help.

❑ Put a smile in your voice.

It only takes a split second to put a smile in your voice. Remember that people hear you smile through the telephone. You should sound warm, friendly and at ease—not rushed and hurried.

❑ Use a well-modulated tone.

Make every effort to speak in a conversational tone. Remember that your voice will project emotions, including anxiety, frustration, irritation, impatience and nonchalance.

❑ Slow your rate of speech.

When you answer the phone sounding rushed and hurried, you may increase the anxiety level of the person who is calling. This causes some customers to question how busy you are and if their call will be handled promptly.

❑ Don't play favorites.

Carefully manage your responses so that one customer doesn't feel less important than another.

I once returned a call to the human resources director of a large healthcare organization. Much to my surprise, the technician who answered the telephone verbalized a unique way of putting me on hold. Here's how our conversation went:

Technician: *Medical Lab. This is Velma.*

Jeannie: *Good morning, Velma. This is Jeannie Davis. I'm returning a call to Virginia Moore.*

Technician: *She's in the lab somewhere. Lemme 'park' your call while I page her.* (click)

Jeannie: *Thank you.*

Yes, the technician was willing to help me by paging Ms. Moore. But, all sorts of thoughts entered my mind. *How do you 'park' a call? Is it legal? Did I call a local hospital or the Department of Transportation? Will I get a ticket if I'm 'parked' too long?*

Most of us are in the habit of asking if the customer will hold. But, rather than wait for an answer to our question, we have a tendency to cut the customer off—usually before we're finished asking the question. To make matters worse, we typically don't wait for a response. Does this sound familiar?

Good afternoon, XYZ Company. Could you hold...? (click)
Thank you for calling XYZ Associates. Will you hold ple...? (click)
XYZ Company. This is Curtis. Can you hold please? (click)

Each situation calls for common sense and a great deal of courtesy. We expect others to respect our phone time. Why shouldn't we respect the hold time of our customers. Most companies receive a large volume of international or intrastate calls and many customers call long distance or from cellular and wireless phones. Some customers don't have time on their side when returning calls between meetings or when using a payphone.

Ask the Customer to Hold

Think of why you ask the customer to hold. Are you typically busy performing other tasks while answering the telephone? Are you simply accustomed to asking the repetitive question and speaking in a monotonous tone? Is there the slightest hint of sincerity in your voice when you raise the question? Do you really care if the customer can hold or not?

> To ask a question and not wait for a response is just plain inconsiderate and rude. Each customer who contacts your company has a reason for doing so, and people expect you to respond with a sense of urgency. Whether or not you demonstrate an ability to do so will impact their first impression.

Imagine your customers standing in the checkout line of a local supermarket. Some are content to patiently wait their turn and others will move to a shorter checkout line. Still others will leave the store and come back at a more convenient time. In any case, most of them don't have to be in line at all. Given a choice, your customers will gladly take their place in line as long as they aren't made to feel as though they must. In other words, people value choice.

In the spirit of customer satisfaction, ask each caller to hold for you. Your customers seldom mind doing something for you. Presumably, you've introduced yourself to the caller in your initial greeting, which helps establish a rapport. Most customers are patient and understanding of your challenge to manage multiple tasks when you come across as genuinely interested and concerned about their reason for calling.

When you ask a customer to hold the line, you're saying:

I respect your telephone time and your reason for contacting our company.
I really want to help you and I don't want you to take your business elsewhere.

Asking the customer to hold for you presents a more personable approach to building a rapport and acknowledging their value to your organization. It demonstrates your commitment to customer satisfaction. It sends a message that you're accountable for this portion of the business relationship, no matter how brief the contact is.

Here are some suggestions for personalizing the hold request:

Are you able to hold for me?
Can you please hold for me?
Will you hold a moment for me?

Using this technique feels differently to the customer—it sounds more personable and friendly and enables the customer to visualize how aware you are of their valuable time.

Wait for a Response

Now that you've taken the first step to gain the customer's respect for your time, reciprocate by waiting for a response from the customer. In most instances, the customer is glad to accommodate your request. Be courteous and give them an opportunity to make an appropriate choice.

More often than not, the customer will respond "yes." Sometimes circumstances beyond your control cause the customer to respond "no."   Whatever the customer's reason: an urgent call, a scheduled telephone appointment, a long distance or mobile call or a previously negative experience with holding—you're responsible for providing an opportunity for the customer to make an appropriate choice.

What do you do when the customer says "no?" Respect the customer's decision not to hold and expedite the call. Immediately obtain the information necessary to handle the call in a timely, efficient manner, even if there are other customers on hold. These requests seldom occur and when they do, you should graciously comply.

What happens when you handle multiple phone lines in a busy office and are unable to wait for a response? A professional, friendly request disguised as an indirect question might be in order. Be certain your smile can be heard as you say:

Hold for me, please.
I will appreciate your holding for me.
Please hold for me; I'll get right back to you.
There is a call before you. Please hold.

Practice this technique using a firm but pleasant vocal tone that doesn't sound rude, abrupt or impersonal.

How Long is too Long

Imagine being in an elevator when the power goes out. You're unable to see what's happening on the other side of the elevator door. The silence and darkness seem to turn seconds into minutes and minutes into hours. You begin asking yourself:

Why did this happen?
Does anybody know I'm here?
How long will I be here?
Is anyone coming to help me?
Have they forgotten about me?
How much longer must I wait?

Customers experience similar feelings of distress and frustration when they're put on hold. They feel helpless, imprisoned, neglected or, even worse, forgotten. Studies show that seven out of ten business callers are placed on hold. Of these, 85% will remain on the line if they hear a message.

A reasonable length of time for customers to be on hold should not exceed 20 to 30 seconds.

Many telephone systems offer a friendly reminder tone (a beep or buzz) to let you know the customer is still on hold. Check to make sure your company's telephone system will activate within the 30-second time frame. Return to the caller within that space of time to give a status update whenever necessary. Be certain to give the customer an option for ending the call or continuing to hold.

Beware of non-productive hold time. Whether you're working with external customers or interdepartmental entities, leaving someone on hold for excessive amounts of time can be costly—eventually impacting your bottom line. Here's a real life example of the impact excessive holding can have on one's workday.

"Hang On" — A Valuable Lesson Learned

Just when I thought I had seen it all, the importance of abusive, non-productive holding came to light while conducting the following classroom exercise:

I asked the audience to close their eyes and then simulated a telephone ringing. I then put the class on "hold," instructing them to open their eyes when they felt they had been on hold long enough.

The objective of the exercise is to help people understand how uncomfortable "holding" is while waiting in total darkness and silence. This exercise never fails to produce a predictable outcome: Most everyone opens their eyes within 30 seconds.

Except, Roslyn! We waited 60 seconds for Roslyn to experience the "enough is enough" feeling as she sat silently in the darkness. Not certain if she had fallen asleep or if she was simply enjoying the quiet time, I announced the exercise was over. She opened her eyes.

Of course, we were eager to understand why she didn't mind being on hold for such a long period of time. Her response: "In my job, I do a lot of research. I call several vendors throughout the day to verify customer account history and to get other information. People regularly place me on hold while gathering the information I need, sometimes for as long as 20 to 25 minutes."

Chapter 5

Messaging:
The Give And Take Of It

Don't assume that voice mail is the only way your customer can effectively communicate a message to someone in your organization. Some customers prefer you write down the message they wish to convey. Therefore, be mindful of what's important when taking handwritten or computer-generated messages.

The Fine Art Of Message Taking

It's easy to understand why customers choose not to leave a voice mail message. Some people believe they'll get a quicker response if you take the message by hand; others believe a computer generated message will be viewed by the recipient in a more timely manner; some simply don't like talking to voice messaging systems.

Sometimes we don't realize the impact a well-written message has on the other person's ability to return a call with confidence. A good team player will recognize the benefit of capturing all relevant information for the call recipient. Your coworkers will appreciate your thoughtfulness and your customers will appreciate your attention to detail.

No matter how often you take verbal messages, it's imperative that you're familiar with the fundamental elements of message taking. After all, voice messaging systems do occasionally fail and computer systems do, too! Reinforce your commitment to customer service excellence by using these tips to enhance your message-taking skills.

Message-Taking Checklist

Think through these questions to check your efficiency at message taking.

		Yes	No
1.	Does your department consistently make use of an "in-and-out" board?	❑	❑
2.	Do you write messages that are difficult to decipher and understand?	❑	❑
3.	Do you go the extra mile to deliver the message in a timely manner?	❑	❑
4.	Do you gather all pertinent details when appropriate?	❑	❑
5.	Do you use callback forms and fill in all the blanks?	❑	❑
6.	Do you misplace messages that have been scribbled on pieces of scratch paper or Post Its?	❑	❑
7.	Do you write legibly?	❑	❑
8.	Do you sign or initial each message?	❑	❑
9.	Do you ask how to spell individual and company names?	❑	❑
10.	Do you verify the information by repeating the message?	❑	❑

"Hide-and-Seek"

Create an "in-and-out" board to keep track of each person in your department. It's important you're knowledgeable and informed about the availability of the person in charge and the whereabouts of your coworkers. Your customers expect to be given timely, accurate information when contacting anyone in your organization.

Remember when you were a child playing the fun game of "hide-and-seek?" Sometimes in the workplace, you can relive those childhood memories when trying to hunt down coworkers—and there's nothing "fun" about it. One of the most challenging work habits to develop is letting others know when you'll be away from your office and when you'll return.

Do you know the whereabouts of people in your workgroup? Do your customers spend an excessive amount of time on hold while you play "hide and seek?" Do you waste valuable time tracking down the call recipient only to find that he or she is in a meeting, gone for the day, at lunch or away for a moment?

Many of us enjoy the autonomy of working in an environment where as adults we come and go as we please. Most of us take full advantage of our "in-and-out" privilege, much to the detriment of others who also play a role in shaping customer perceptions. What image do you project when offering customer responses such as:

She was just here a minute ago; I don't know where she went.
I think he's out of the office today. Let me check for you.
Hang on. I'll see if I can find him.
She didn't say where she was going. I'll transfer you to voice mail.
I don't think he's back yet.

Embarrassing? You bet! Time and time again, workshop participants share stories of missed appointments, untimely callbacks, lost commissions or worse, because no one knew where they were or messages were not delivered in a timely manner.

Discuss with the person in charge of your workgroup the value of creating an "in-and-out" board. Then have some fun playing "hide-and-seek" by exploring creative ways to penalize those who don't make consistent use of your "in-and-out" tracking system. Each person can and should be held accountable for letting others know their whereabouts, for example: One of our clients implemented a "pay-as-you-go" policy. Whenever someone left the office without noting their out-of-office status on the board, they were required to contribute $1.00 in the departmental "come-and-go-if-you-dare" box. Everyone had fun catching each other in the act. Within a week, the group collected enough money to purchase a cake and refreshments to celebrate a team member's birthday. It wasn't long before the group expanded the rules to collect a $1.00 contribution from teammates who remembered to check out but forgot to let anyone know they had returned.

Use Callback Forms

Make sure you have easy access to callback forms. Letting the customer know you "need to get something to write on, or with," is unacceptable. Jotting notes on scratch paper or Post Its isn't the best way to show your concern for the customer's reason for calling. You want teammates to feel confident every time they return a call.

Fill in all the blanks when using callback forms to record incoming calls. Carefully make note of the date, time, area code and nature of the call. Write legibly and sign or initial each message. You want the person returning the call to know you've documented all information with care.

Carbonized callback forms offer a great way to recall relevant information, track incoming call volume, develop a customer database and more. Imagine you've delivered the message and the call is returned, but no contact is made. You'll be glad you have an extra copy of the message on hand after you learn the callback slip was accidentally thrown away or misplaced.

Spell Names Correctly

One's name is the most useful tool a person has, and its sound is just as important. No one wants his or her name mispronounced or misspelled on correspondence. And as we all know, a misspelled name input into a computer system can become incorrect information eternally committed to a computer's memory. Correcting computer-generated information in permanent records presents a challenge because it seems there's little chance for correction.

Save time and energy by asking for the appropriate spelling of your customer's name. Minimize embarrassing situations by letting the customer know you want to make certain you've spelled the name correctly. It's also a good idea to ask for the correct spelling of corporate names, addresses and acronyms as well. Phrase your request as follows:

Please spell your name for me; I want to be sure I get it right.
It's important I spell your company's name correctly. Please spell it for me.
Is that an acronym? It would be helpful if you would spell it for me.

Years ago, it was customary to ask for the correct spelling of a customer's last name only. Today, people have a unique way of spelling first names. We often assume the traditional spelling of first names, without giving any thought to the creativity of parents. I've met many people who have creative spellings for their names, for example:

Jac	(Jack)	Jenne	(Ginny)
Khyme	(Kim)	Aimee	(Amy)
Bobbye	(Bobby)	Jeanne	(Jeannie)
Larance	(Lawrence)	Micheal	(Michael)

If your customer's first or last name is difficult to spell or pronounce, do yourself a favor and ask the correct spelling. Ask the customer to say his or her name slowly, so you can hear the name clearly and distinctly.

When the name is difficult to pronounce, ask the person to pronounce the name for you. Then (in parentheses) write the name phonetically, sounding out each syllable, for example: Katherin Kaufie (Kath – er – in - Koff – ee).

Using this technique enables everyone in your organization to return calls with confidence. Imagine what a great first impression you'll make when you pronounce a customer's name correctly. Here's an exercise that reinforces the need to spell the customer's name correctly and phonetically:

What's In A Name?

Can you think of ten ways to spell Catherine Koffie?
More than 2,016 spelling combinations exist.

Example:

Katherin Coffee	**Catheryn Kawfy**
Catherine Coughee	**Kathryn Caufee**
Kathryn Koffie	**Cathryn Kaufie**

1. _____   6. _____

2. _____   7. _____

3. _____   8. _____

4. _____   9. _____

5. _____   10. _____

Repeat the Message

Be certain to repeat each message for the caller. Make every effort to convey the message as it's given. Remember that miscommunication can occur when we attempt to interpret our customer's language.

Some customers leave lengthy voice mail messages that allow them to outline every detail of their reason for calling. When taking handwritten messages, politely ask the customer to provide a brief summary then repeat the message to make sure you wrote it correctly. You may need to paraphrase comments or abbreviate a few words. In any case, be cautious not to downplay the relevance of key points.

It's easy to inadvertently transpose numbers. Take the time to verify all telephone numbers, area codes, times, dates and other numerical information. Make any necessary corrections and again repeat those numbers to the caller for further verification. Ask productive questions to verify key points that ensure your clear understanding of the customer's message.

Deliver the Message

How effective is your company's message retrieval system? Is there a sense of urgency to deliver messages in a timely manner? Do you post messages in a convenient central location? Do you willingly go the extra mile when you notice the call recipient has not yet picked up a message?

Make a special effort to deliver the message when you take a break or before going out for lunch. Or place a friendly reminder call so the call recipient remembers to pick up the message. Whatever you do, don't just leave the message in a hole. Of course, you know depositing handwritten messages or notes on chairs, computer screens or cluttered desktops can equal frustration for everyone involved.

Whenever possible, think of reasonable alternatives for delivering customer messages without delay. Consider sending an e-mail message on behalf of the customer or take time to leave a voice mail message for the call recipient. Sometimes you have an opportunity to re-route the call or handle it yourself. If you're able to respond to a customer's immediate need, keep the call recipient informed. Let the person know what action was taken with the call and when it occurred. Doing so takes the guesswork out of "Whatever happened to...?"

Avoid Awkward Responses

An unpolished response leaves a negative impression with the caller. Remember that you're presenting an image of your company. When the person called is unavailable, be certain to offer an appropriate response. In the spirit of teamwork, take care not to share personal information about your peers or give the impression you work in a dysfunctional organization.

It seems we spend more time in business meetings than we do in our offices and we meet ourselves coming and going. To continuously say, "He or she is in a meeting" leaves much to the customer's imagination. Let the caller know immediately when the person called is unavailable and why. When appropriate, you might say: "He's meeting with our sales staff now... or "She's meeting with a client now...."

Give the customer a general idea when the person called can be reached, for instance, say: "Cindy is out of the office this morning. I expect her to return around 3 p.m." or "She is expected to be away several hours...." Don't make the mistake of saying, "She'll be in later this afternoon." The caller is sure to ask for an exact time and will expect a return call promptly.

Some time ago, I returned a call to the training director of a manufacturing company. I'd never spoken to her nor had I ever met her. Yet, the person who accepted the call informed me: "She went over to Saint Joseph's Hospital to have some tests done. If she does come back today, she probably won't feel like talking to anybody. I think it's best you call back tomorrow."

I truthfully didn't know what to think. I was certain the ailing person would have been disappointed to know this personal information was being shared with strangers. What do you think?

Check out these responses then test your skill at completing this three-in-one exercise.

Avoid Awkward Responses
(Part I and II)

Check any comment you've heard before, then indicate
why the response is inappropriate and provide a better response.

Inappropriate   **Why?**

❏ He's on break right now.   _____

❏ She hasn't come in yet.   _____

❏ She's tied up right now.   _____

❏ He's still not back.   _____

❏ Ms. Wilson's desk.   _____

❏ Can you call back later?   _____

❏ He took his kid to the doctor. _____

❏ He's out sick today.   _____

❏ She had a doctor's appointment. _____

Avoid Awkward Responses
(Part III)

Write a better response that will convey a positive image for your
company or workgroup.

1. _____

2. _____

3. _____

4. _____

5. _____

6. _____

7. _____

8. _____

9. _____

10. _____

Work to increase your awareness of awkward responses. Think before you speak and
visualize the reaction to each response the customer receives.

Friendly Reminders:

➤ Be prepared to take handwritten messages. Don't indicate a reluctance to do so.

➤ Take well-written messages that enable others to return a call with confidence.

➤ Fill in all the blanks. Carefully note the time, date, area code, phone number and message.

➤ Stop playing "hide-and-seek." Create an "in-and-out" board and have fun implementing ways of encouraging everyone's participation.

➤ Use callback forms instead of pieces of scratch paper or Post Its. Consider the usefulness of carbonized callback forms.

➤ Don't hesitate to ask for correct spelling of individual or company names.

➤ Write names correctly and phonetically when they're difficult to pronounce.

➤ Summarize and repeat the message for every caller. Verify all numerical references and be careful not to transpose numbers.

➤ Go the extra mile to deliver messages. Don't just put messages in the "hole" or leave them on chairs or computer screens.

➤ Break the "He- or She-is-in-a-meeting" automatic response. Your customer will appreciate a more personable response, i.e., with whom, how long, expected return.

➤ When responding to customers, be sure not to divulge personal information about coworkers.

➤ Let the customer know immediately the person called is unavailable or away from their office.

➢ Substitute the word "office" for "desk." A desk is a piece of furniture; an office is a professional workspace, suite, department or building.

➢ Avoid suggesting the person "call back later." You don't want to appear disinterested or unconcerned.

➢ Work out a system for keeping track of people. To say, "I don't know where he is" indicates lack of knowledge and/or cooperation within your company.

Chapter 6

Voice Messaging:
A Condiment For Business Success

A condiment for business success? You may question this analogy, but consider the many improvements and variations of each condiment as it relates to meeting the individual taste of hot dog lovers. Just like the zest and flavor catsup, mustard, relish and onion bring to the all-American hotdog, voice messaging features offer a similar opportunity to spice up what would otherwise be a very generic voice messaging system.

Technology, with all its bells and whistles, is the condiment of telephone communications and, although we sometimes resist its affect on our lives, where would we be without it? Voice messaging has become the common way to exchange information in the business world. You can save valuable time and avoid playing telephone tag if you learn how to use voice messaging more effectively.

Years ago, we asked customers, "Do you have a fax machine?" Today we simply ask, "What's your fax number." And today, "Call me," is followed by, "If I'm not in just leave the info on my voice mail." And think about this, when was the last time you heard a busy signal in corporate America? Voice messaging is everywhere and is used by practically everyone. And because our business needs are different, voice messaging systems can be made to suit individual tastes—just like our favorite hotdog.

The notion of voice messaging began with the concept of answering machines and it continues to incorporate features that improve ease of use and practicality for all. We've become accustomed to the many condiments that go well with voice messaging systems, such as:

- ◆ Individual voice mailboxes
- ◆ Pre-recorded messages
- ◆ Remote message retrieval
- ◆ Message notification
- ◆ Extended absence greetings
- ◆ Message waiting indicators
- ◆ Extensive message retention
- ◆ Automatic play-back features
- ◆ Easy-to-skip message capabilities

- ◆ Instant reply without dialing the telephone
- ◆ Messages deleted on command
- ◆ Message forwarding to others in your system
- ◆ Erase and re-record features
- ◆ Normal and urgent message prompts
- ◆ Menu options
- ◆ Call routing features
- ◆ Computer voice mail
- ◆ Detailed messages

Some companies don't have voice messaging systems. Many believe this technology eliminates personal customer interaction and thus customers might resent talking to an automated system. Yet, most people are accustomed to transacting business via voice mail. You may want to consider installing a voice messaging system when you notice how frequently customers say:

> *Does he have voice mail?*
> *Can I leave her a voice mail message?*
> *I'll just leave her a voice mail message.*
> *Transfer me to his voice mail.*

Could it be that your customers are accustomed to the use of voice messaging as an effective business communication tool? Monitor the responses of customers who appreciate the personal attention provided when a "live" person answers the telephone. Then make note of those who request access to voice mail. Any surprises?

Many of us share a love-hate relationship with voice mail. We love being available to receive messages, even when we are unavailable. But, we hate pressing menu options and not speaking to a "live" person. Such is the downside of voice messaging systems, but they are effective business communication tools and we need to use them.

Think of how you can use voice messaging to enhance your telephone communication skills. Successful voice mail users view this technology as an asset when working with others on the telephone. And most customers view effective voice mail users as committed professionals who are efficient, responsive and well-organized. Ineffective voice mail habits can alter customer perceptions, jeopardize customer relationships, hamper your ability to be productive, reveal disorganized work habits and encourage telephone tag.

Using Your Voice Messaging System

Learning to make the best use of your voice messaging system can be quite challenging. Sometimes we don't realize how communication skills impact our productivity when using voice messaging systems. We often make the assumption that as long as the customer can leave a message, everything is A-O-K. The following voice mail tips will boost your productivity while enhancing customer relationships.

Call Yourself!

Make certain your message sounds inviting, not monotonous, canned, or impersonal. Practice recording your message until you sound relaxed and comfortable or until you can deliver your message in a conversational tone.

It's important your smile can be heard in the message. Just because customers can't speak with you directly, doesn't mean they expect you to demonstrate less interest and concern for their call. The tone of your message should be upbeat, conveying the same professionalism and pleasant expression you expect when calling others.

Speak at a slower pace to avoid sounding robotic, rushed or hurried. Be certain to state your name, company or department and important instructions for the listener in an easy-to-understand manner. It isn't unusual for customers to redial your telephone number because the message is spoken too quickly, instructions are unclear, and you sound as though you're rambling or you mumbled instead of carefully enunciating each word.

Make a mental note to call yourself and listen to your message. If what you hear doesn't convey the image you want, change your message.

Ask for Specific Information

Make a habit of asking the caller to leave their name, telephone number and, if appropriate, their reason for calling. Frequent callers sometimes assume you have easy access to their contact information and often will not leave their telephone number. This can be frustrating because there are times you may not have the number readily available, especially when you return business calls from a remote location or car phone.

Sometimes the game of telephone tag is initiated as a result of customers leaving incomplete messages. If all you need is a little bit of information, say so in the recording by asking the caller to "leave a brief message."

Ask callers to leave a "detailed message" whenever specific information would be more helpful. In most instances, you'll be able to respond appropriately when returning their call, even if you need to leave a voice mail message in response.

It's not considered impolite to ask callers to speak slowly when leaving their message. Too often, we may need to replay a message several times before capturing pertinent information. You might say:

Please record your message slowly so that
I can make note of relevant details.

Update Your Voice Mail Greeting

Voice mail is a communication tool used to let others know your availability. Changing your voice mail greeting frequently is not difficult or time consuming. To do so demonstrates your willingness to let customers know you're eager to serve them and that their call really is important to you and your company.

Some businesses consistently use a standard message. Unfortunately, some customers view standard messages as impersonal or unfriendly. Consider recording daily voice mail messages that include the date and other pertinent daily information. Using this technique informs callers of your in-or-out status and gives them a realistic idea of when you might return their call.

Remember to change your message while on vacation or if you plan to be away from the office for more than a few hours. Be mindful to record a message that gives the customer an idea of when you will return, when they can expect to hear back from you and when they can call again to speak with you. To leave a lengthy, detailed itinerary on your recorded message doesn't tell the customer anything, except that you're probably too busy to handle their business.

A sure way to aggravate your customers is to leave the standard "I'm-either-on-another-line-or-away-from-my-desk" message, especially when you're out of the office due to an unexpected illness. How many times have you heard this message and pressed "0" for assistance, only to discover the person you're calling is out of the office attending a two-day seminar?

When you make a habit of updating your message, you'll save yourself a lot of embarrassment. I once called someone and got the following voice mail message:

> *This is Keith. I'll be on vacation until May 25th. Please leave a message*
> *at the sound of the tone and I'll return your call when I get back.*

The problem? I placed my call on May 27th, and Keith still hadn't updated his voice mail message!

Provide a Live-Person Option

Make your message user friendly. When appropriate, provide instructional information on how customers can reach a "live" person. You might say:

I will be unavailable most of today and look forward to returning your call as soon as possible. If you need immediate assistance, press "0" and Edward will redirect your call.

Whenever possible, let the customer know who they can speak with in your absence. Your customers appreciate knowing who can help them if you're away for an extended length of time. Leave the person's name, phone number or extension on your recorded message, for example:

*Gerri will be glad to help you in my absence.
She can be reached on extension 235.*

Adjust the "Ring" Cycle

Forward incoming calls directly to your voice messaging system. This way, your phone will be answered after one ring, instead of four or five. Your customers anticipate the need to leave a voice mail message when your telephone rings more than a few times, but they don't want to wait through the ring cycle and your answering phrase before they can leave a message of their own.

It's a good idea to use this technique when you're away from the office for any length of time or when you'd like to minimize interruptions. You can be more productive when you're meeting with others in your office or working to meet a deadline if you forward calls to the voice messaging system.

Follow the "Sundown" Rule

Nine out of ten voice mail complaints relate to "slow response." You need to go the extra mile and treat callers with the same respect and common courtesy you expect from them. So follow the "sundown" rule by making every effort to return all calls by the end of each day.

Think of a time when you've left several voice mail messages for someone who didn't return your call or didn't return it timely. How many people did you tell? Most likely, you're not alone. Others may share the same frustration with this individual and they'll tell people, too. As a result, someone earns a bad reputation. Don't let it be you!

Be certain to check your voice mail at regular intervals. Make sure to complete whatever research is necessary before you return a customer's call. It's non-productive to retrieve a detailed message and return the call when you're unprepared to respond appropriately. Unless, of course, you return the call to acknowledge receipt of the message and you commit to calling again once you can appropriately respond.

Time-management experts recommend setting aside an hour a day to make and return your phone calls. Most people are in the office and accessible by telephone during the first two hours of the morning and the last two hours of the afternoon. True, during the course of a workday, we seem to meet ourselves coming and going and meetings take up a lot of our time, but we owe it to our customers to be responsive.

Make a conscious effort to set aside time for returning calls. If time is short, designate a half-hour in the morning and the same amount of time in the afternoon to place your calls. Create a system for returning calls that works for you and stick to it.

One of our clients, a supervisor who receives as many as 30 voice mail messages a day, felt overwhelmed at the thought of managing callbacks in a timely manner. As a result, customers complained regularly, questioned the effective operation of her department and began to call others for information in order to circumvent leaving yet another unanswered message.

Listen carefully to each message as you play it. Sometimes skipping through messages can cause you to miss important details, specific deadlines and time frames to which the caller needs a response. If necessary, return calls at the end of your workday. Sometimes it's better to leave a message of acknowledgement than it is not to return calls at all.

Make this simple callback system work for you:

❑ Return calls immediately to those whose messages require a simple "yes" or "no" response.

❑ Immediately return calls to those who can be helped by someone else or referred to another individual or department. Be certain to give the person's name and correct contact information.

❑ Take notes for calls that require specific information so you can respond to each topic when returning the call. Do what you can to eliminate the need for a customer to call back because your response is incomplete.

❑ If necessary, call back after work to make sure the customer hears your response first thing in the morning.

❑ Place calls to coworkers responsible for retrieving information relevant to an appropriate reply. Let them know you'll appreciate a prompt response.

❑ Forward the customer's message directly to someone who can help. Request their prompt attention to the matter in your introduction of the transferred message. Call the customer to let them know with whom they should follow-up.

❑ Acknowledge messages from those who require specific information and commit to call again within a designated time frame if you need to research their request.

❑ Make time to call people with whom you don't want to talk. Call after work if you must, but return their call. Thank them for contacting you and let them know you're not interested, if that's the case.

There's absolutely no excuse for not responding! When people take time out of their busy day to contact you, extend them the not-so-common-courtesy of returning their call. Your thoughtfulness and timely response will speak volumes about the value you place on customer satisfaction.

Leaving A Voice Mail Message

Imagine your ability to conduct everyday business effectively without talking to a single person on the phone and getting positive results. Leaving a voice mail message is not simply a matter of saying "This is Faye. Call me back when you get a chance." There are many other factors to consider.

Vocal Quality

How do you sound? When leaving messages, it's important that you sound like you. Put some enthusiasm in your voice. Think of how you feel when people leave you a message that sounds as though they didn't really want to call but had no choice.

Your vocal tone has a lot to do with how others perceive your attitude and can account for more than 80% of your impact on the telephone, both when answering calls and when leaving messages. Your challenge is to create an image customers will remember with pleasure even though they can't see you. When you speak in a natural tone, you sound confident, friendly and conversational.

You want to sound interesting and enthusiastic, not overly anxious, bored or monotonous. Vary your pitch using a well-modulated tone. Using inflection in your voice can get the other person excited about the reason for your call. If you're unable to display a positive attitude before leaving a voice mail message, place the call at another time.

Pay close attention to volume. It should be easy to listen to your voice. Be careful not to speak too loudly or too quietly. If the listener needs to hold the phone away from his or her ear because you're talking at the top of your lungs, important details can be missed.

If you're soft-spoken, be certain your voice is audible—more than a whisper. You don't want listening to be a strain. Whatever the scenario, the recipient shouldn't find it necessary to repeatedly play your message to understand what's being said.

Be mindful of your rate of speech. We've all experienced listening in amazement to messages that are left at a pace faster than the speed of sound. We're understandably frustrated when we need to replay a message several times in order to understand what the caller said. Fast talkers have a tendency to run words and phrases together, sounding jumbled, rushed or hurried. Vocal quality suffers when you aren't careful to speak at a rate of speech that can be easily understood.

Many voice messaging systems allow you to review your recorded message before sending it. Whenever possible, listen to your message. If necessary, re-record and listen again. Does your message convey exactly the image you want the caller to perceive? And is your message conveyed clearly?

Remember to keep a mirror handy. It will serve as a friendly reminder to put the smile in your voice as you record your message.

Clarity

Details are important. Leave messages that don't require a return call. Make every effort to record a message that can be understood the first time it's heard. Clearly state your name, company and phone number at the beginning of the message.

Spell it out. If your name or company name is difficult to pronounce, say the name slowly so the recipient can pronounce the name correctly when returning your call. In some instances, you may need to spell your first and last name for the recipient; don't assume the listener will know correct name spellings. As with names of streets, cities and other relevant information, your willingness to help by providing the correct spelling ensures a properly recorded message.

Using this technique will save valuable time. Suppose your voice message doesn't require a verbal response and the recipient can reply by sending information in the mail at your request. If you don't spell names on the message, there's a good possibility the correspondence will be addressed incorrectly. We all know how hard it is to have corrections made once information has been entered into a database.

Date and time please. It's a good idea to let the recipient know the date and time of your message. Many voice messaging systems allow the recipient to verify this information within their system. However, you can save the recipient a few steps by stating the date and time of your call. This technique is especially helpful when your reason for calling is time sensitive.

Leave your phone number. Make a habit of recording your phone number on the message, even if you're calling a person with whom you have frequent contact. This is another time-saver. There will be instances when the recipient retrieves voice messages from a remote location and may not have easy access to your telephone number, which can cause delays in timely callbacks.

Say your phone number slowly, carefully pausing between area code, prefix and the last four digits. It takes people longer to process auditory messages, so it's helpful to say the phone number in pairs, rather than single digits. You might say:

My telephone number is (pause) area code 7-7-0 (pause) 4-3-7 (pause) 53 (pause) 26.

When you use this technique, the likelihood of mistaking one number for another will decrease significantly. Chances are the recipient is less likely to transpose the numbers, resulting in fewer misdialed calls.

When leaving a rather lengthy message, leave your name and phone number both at the beginning of the message and at the end. This will allow the recipient an opportunity to write down your name and number at the beginning of the message and to confirm it at the end.

Brief and Concise

Why are you calling? Know what you want to accomplish with the call. Record clear, rational, and thoughtful information in your message. Too many times, we hastily launch into lengthy monologue without regard for who the listener is or how the person will benefit from our call. An effective voice mail message will include a succinct subject and every request for action should be carefully conveyed in your message.

Record details of your reason for calling in a format that is brief and concise. The optimum length of a normal message should not exceed 20 to 30 seconds. You don't want to risk being disconnected in mid-sentence and you surely don't want to call back in order to finish recording your message. To do so is likely to agitate the recipient and result in a delayed callback.

How much is too much? Some of us think more is better. We attempt to record a single message that covers several topics. Then we're frustrated when the recipient fails to acknowledge each item requested. Limit your recorded message to one or two topics. This provides the recipient an opportunity to forward messages to other users who may be able to respond appropriately. If your message extends beyond one minute, you may want to consider an alternative method of delivery.

If you must incorporate several topics into one voice mail message, make certain to enumerate every point. This enables call recipients to make note of each topic and appropriately tailor their reply. Sometimes it's beneficial to send a fax message instead of leaving a lengthy recorded message.

Organization

Don't just improvise. Be prepared to record your message. Most of us don't expect to hear the voice of a "live" person on the other end of the phone. After a few rings, we generally anticipate the need to leave a voice mail message, yet are frequently unprepared to do so when we hear the beep!

Leaving incomplete messages is a great way to initiate a game of telephone tag! If you're uncertain about specific details, make every effort to clear up the matter before you place the call. Do whatever it takes to eliminate an unnecessary callback from the recipient.

Prioritize your thoughts. Miscommunication can occur when you bounce from topic to topic without regard for the recipient's need to receive clear, concise messages that can be acted upon in a timely manner.   Make every effort to convey pertinent information that can be easily understood. Take a few seconds to review any material relevant to your reason for calling. Jot down notes about your topic, specific requests for action and expected outcomes. Highlight key points before you begin recording your message. Speak from your notes and checkmark every topic to be certain you've explained all details.

Record special instructions early in the message. You don't want to risk the recipient skipping over your message if a critical deadline needs to be met. Is there something you forgot to say that could impact a timely callback? Consider using this checklist for special instructions:

❑ Ask the recipient to leave a reply in your absence, either in your voice mailbox or with someone else.

❑ Give the recipient an idea when you'll be available for a callback.

❑ Give specific time frames for when you need a reply and why, if appropriate.

❑ Let recipients know what time you'll call again and ask them to confirm their availability.

❑ Leave appropriate contact information if others are involved.

❑ Prioritize requests for action.

Voice Mail Pitfalls

Bad news travels fast! Negative messages sent via your voice messaging system can end up being detrimental to you. Be certain that any message you send is one you don't mind sharing with others. Such messages could send the wrong signal to the recipient and can easily be forwarded to a third party. You'll minimize the risk of embarrassing yourself and others when you give thoughtful, careful consideration to every message you send, including those marked personal or confidential.

Is your call really urgent? Carefully evaluate the urgency of your call and don't abuse the urgent-message delivery option. You don't want to be perceived as the "boy who cried wolf." Only use this feature when immediate review of the message content is critical. Think about other alternatives for contacting the person. Did they leave a pager number on their recorded message? Can you press "0" to get immediate assistance? Did they leave the name and number of someone else who could help?

Speakerphones. Are you inclined to leave messages using the convenience of a speakerphone? If so, keep in mind that poor voice quality can misrepresent the image you want to project. You may come across as muffled or garbled and you certainly don't want to sound as though you're calling from deep inside an underground well.

Mobile flexibility—It's your dime! It seems everyone is on the go these days. Some of us do a great job of returning calls from wireless, cellular or pay phones. Whatever your method of communicating with others, consider the quality of your call. If you're mobile, place calls when reception is clearest. If there are breaks or static on the line, your message may not be understandable or heard at all. Avoid causing the recipient to fill-in-the-blanks or guess at telephone numbers and other information. If necessary, delete the message and call again when there is little or no noise or interference.

Voice messaging is a powerful business communication tool. Learning to use the features of your voice messaging system will help you become more efficient and productive when interacting with your customers. Improving your telephone communication skills and developing good voice mail habits will enhance customer relationships and keep you ahead of the pack.

Friendly Reminders:

<u>Do</u>:	<u>Do Not</u>:

<u>Do</u>:

➤ Call yourself!

➤ Ask for specific information.

➤ Update your voice mail greeting regularly.

➤ Leave your name and phone number.

➤ Provide a live-person option.

➤ Forward incoming calls directly to voice mail when necessary.

➤ Follow the "sundown" rule.

➤ Record clear, rational and thoughtful information.

➤ Record special instructions early in your message.

➤ Retrieve messages frequently.

<u>Do Not</u>:

➤ Leave lengthy voice mail messages.

➤ Sound monotonous, canned or impersonal.

➤ Speak too fast or too loudly.

➤ Leave incomplete messages.

➤ Abuse the urgent-message delivery option.

➤ Record an "I'm-either-on-another line-or-away-from-my-desk" message.

➤ Skip over messages; you could miss something important.

➤ Leave rambling voice mail messages.

➤ Leave negative, personal or confidential messages.

➤ Play telephone tag.

Chapter 7

"People who fight fire with fire usually end up with ashes."
– Abigail Van Buren

Handling Complaint Callers:
Profit Opportunities With A Twist

Complaint callers present profit opportunities. View a complaint call as a chance to increase the value of your product or service, to improve the operation of your business, to strengthen customer relationships and to enhance customer service. Successful businesses encourage complaints and criticisms, and they act upon them in a timely manner.

It's unrealistic to think the customer is always right. The reality is that the customer is always the customer. When it comes to pleasing customers, it doesn't matter whether they're right or wrong. What matters most is understanding the behaviors associated with handling the complaint caller and solving their problem. Customers are your greatest assets and you want each one to value their relationship with your company. Attitude is perhaps the most important characteristic in handling complaint callers—not just the attitude of the person taking the call, but the corporate attitude as well. For example, every organization needs to encourage its people to be sensitive to customer complaints and their impact on the bottom line.

- Does your company have a system in place for dealing with complaint calls?

- Do you have a personal complaint call strategy?

- When you handle complaint calls, does your attitude reflect the corporate philosophy?

- Are you empowered by your organization to resolve complaints quickly and conveniently?

The answers to these questions are important because your complaint call attitude can make or break a long-standing business relationship. Your actions, positive or negative, will impact the overall perception customers have about your company's ethics, products and services.

The manner in which you handle complaint calls is critical. The best marketing, public relations and advertising executives will agree that word-of-mouth promotion can play a significant role in the success of any business. Customer growth and retention depend on it; it influences new product development and enhancement; and, customer service and marketing strategies are built upon it.

Your customers tell at least five others about their positive experiences. They tell ten or more people about their negative experiences. And remember that in business, no news isn't necessarily good news. Some customers may choose not to complain—but to simply stop doing business with you!

At some point in time, most of us have taken our business elsewhere as a result of poorly handled complaint calls. As you recall such an instance in your personal life, think of how your emotions impacted the decision to continue doing business with XYZ Company—or to give their competitor a try. Did you make your decision based on poor customer service, unresolved complaints, untimely handling of complaints or unsatisfactory resolution? What were your feelings about the person handling your call—and about the company? Do you remember how many people you told about your negative experience?

◆ Make it easy for customers to voice complaints. Conduct customer satisfaction surveys, set up a toll-free number and invite complaints and criticisms.

◆ Be responsive. Commit to resolving complaint calls promptly. Provide professional, courteous service and follow-up.

Behavior Styles

Remember that customer satisfaction is your number one objective. Your attitude and knowledge about your company and its products or services are important factors in handling complaint callers. More importantly, the behavior you demonstrate while interacting with your customer can influence a positive outcome. Your challenge is to move beyond the emotionally charged elements of every call in order to solve the customer's problem. Consider how each of the following behavior styles impacts your ability to handle complaint callers.

Childlike Behavior

We demonstrate a variety of childlike behaviors to express feelings of pleasure or pain. We celebrate positive experiences through behavior that conveys joy, laughter, smiles or appreciation. Unpleasant circumstances can cause us to display behaviors associated with tears, anger, frustration or rebellion. Even as adults, our natural defense against adverse circumstances is typically a demonstration of negative childlike behavior. Adopting the childlike behavior style is the most common way to let others know how you feel—it best expresses your emotions.

Demonstrations of childlike behavior typically convey your feelings at the moment—positive or negative. Feelings that can be heard in the sound of your voice; feelings that can either fuel the fire of anger or calm the raging sea; feelings that can transmit negative messages—without regard for the consequences of your actions. It's the behavior style that says:

Negative	**Positive**
I don't care	I'm understanding
I'm defensive	I'm apologetic
I'm sad	I'm happy
I'm frustrated	I'm empathetic
I'm not interested	I'm concerned

In most situations, the best offense is not always a good defense! Make every effort to adopt a positive emotional posture when confronted by a complaint caller. Don't add fuel to the fire by demonstrating negative childlike behavior. You don't want to appear defensive or irresponsible—nor do you want to sound like a whiner.

Whenever you catch yourself making the following remarks (or similar ones), immediately adjust your behavior. Make certain to adopt behaviors that reflect a positive attitude when dealing with adverse circumstances. To do so will reinforce your awareness of the impact negative childlike behavior has on customer relationships. Do these remarks sound familiar?

I wasn't even here that day!
It's not my fault!
You told me to do it that way!
I don't know how it got screwed up!
I didn't do it; she did!

Learn to take responsibility for your actions. Blaming others and offering irrational excuses for your behavior (or someone else's) is inappropriate. Remember that you're accountable for the customer relationship—even if you're on the phone for a brief moment. Be thoughtful and considerate as you listen carefully to what the caller is saying.

Caution! A demonstration of negative childlike behavior typically invites a response that demonstrates parental behavior.

Be careful not to set the stage for a battle that can escalate into war. Stop... think... listen... think. Adopt a behavioral style that will compliment the respectable person you are.

Parental Behavior

People who demonstrate parental behavior are typically perceived as judgmental and self-righteous. It's the one behavior style that leaves no question as to who is right and who is wrong!

Some of us demonstrate parental behavior when working with customers. We assume our posture on every issue is right because of the skills, knowledge and expertise we bring to our jobs. Sometimes we can become too comfortable in our work-related positions and unknowingly take for granted the value of customer relationships. We believe we know our jobs better than anyone else does and are often reluctant to view customer complaints from a different perspective. Well, there are two sides to every story.

An unhappy customer can exhibit parental behavior while voicing their complaint. They want you to listen to their concern and understand their perspective on the relevant issues involved. Many customers don't want their money back—they want a product or service that works! And most of them are willing to settle for far less than you're willing to concede in an effort to satisfy their need.

Like most parents, customers don't want you to question or challenge their expectations of excellent customer service. They hold you accountable for your actions—and sometimes the actions of others. They point the finger at you and expect you'll accept the blame. What they really want is for you to treat them with respect and give them more than they expect. They want the experience of dealing with you and your company to be pleasant.

Classroom discussions on the subject of parental behavior bring back a lot of memories for our workshop participants. During one session, I requested everyone develop a list of parental behavior statements they remember hearing as children. The results were not surprising, making it easier to understand why we can demonstrate negative childlike behavior when customers assume the parental role.

The example I shared with the class involved my father's words: "Jeannie, the way I see it—which is the way that it is...." Some of their examples were:

Speak when you're spoken to; answer when you're called.
Don't you talk back to me.
Shut up and listen to what I'm saying.
Do as I say; not as I do.
I taught you better than that.
You better respect your elders.
Never forget that I'm the parent; you're the child.

These and similar statements come into play when our customers demonstrate parental behavior. We're quick to rebel against their chastising and judgmental remarks. You hear parental behavior when the customer says:

Can't you do anything right?
If you'd pay attention you'd know!
You obviously don't understand!
I'll assume this won't happen again.

Some customers are quick to identify the error of your ways—making you feel like a scolded three-year-old—often without regard for your feelings or emotions. You don't like their in-your-face-attitude. You don't like feeling as though you've been smacked on the back of the hand.

Make every attempt not to internalize what the customer says. Their angry behavior may not be directed toward you, even though you're the person with whom they're speaking. Most likely, it's related to some level of dissatisfaction involving their experience with your product, service or someone else in your organization.

> Caution! A demonstration of parental behavior typically invites a negative child-like response.

The manner in which you respond or react toward customers who demonstrate parental behavior will depend on the kind of behavior style you choose to use.

Adult Behavior

Wouldn't you know it! There's another alternative—a behavioral style that focuses on the more important need to maintain and retain customer relationships. Adult behavior demonstrates your ability to acknowledge problems, analyze them and solve them—quickly and without fanfare. It's the behavioral style that says:

It doesn't matter who screwed it up. Let's fix it—make it right.

*I understand your frustration—and I don't blame you for feeling the way you do.
Here's what we can do to rectify the situation.*

*We value your business and appreciate your concern.
I'll do my best to make sure the problem doesn't reoccur.*

I want to completely understand your concern. I'm sure we can solve your problem.

*What are your expected outcomes for resolution?
I'll do everything I can to accommodate your request(s).*

*Your satisfaction with our products and service is what's important.
Tell me what it will take to make you happy.*

Listen to your customer and keep an open mind. Imagine their problem or concern is real and put yourself in their shoes. Search for common ground, proposing a fair and equitable resolution to their problem. If you're unable to help the customer, find someone who can handle the complaint.

Ask yourself: "What's the customer's specific need and how can I provide it?" Make every effort to find the profit opportunity that can result from solving their problem. Can it lead to a policy change that will affect customer service or marketing efforts? Can it lead to new product development or enhancement? Can it lead to better communications within your department or interdepartmentally? Can it generate an idea for greater efficiency that would improve productivity?

Think of the advantages positive outcomes produce for you and the company. Work to become a problem solver by putting emotions and judgments aside. Concentrate on analyzing the facts of a situation and creating a solution that is practical and beneficial for all.

> Caution! A demonstration of adult behavior can result in you and the customer playing to win.

Playing to win is much different than creating a win-win or win-lose situation. It gives you an opportunity to use every resource you have to be the best you can be. It reaffirms the customer's belief in your organization. It encourages continued long-term working relationships that impact your bottom line.

Climbing The Mountain Of Anger

No service provider likes to hear anger and abuse over the telephone. In most instances, customers are angry when they place their call—they've already climbed to the top of the mountain of anger!

The "mountain of anger" is an analogy I use in workshops and seminars to help others gain a better understanding of complaint call behavior from the customer's perspective. It illustrates the relationship between dissatisfied customers, their supporters, complaint resolution and you. The activities that occur on the mountain of anger will reflect your company's corporate attitude and can create a positive relationship with the customer.

If your phone calls are prescreened, you may be forewarned that a disgruntled customer is on the line, which gives you adequate time to prepare for the call. But what if the caller arrives uninvited and unannounced? Your positioning on the mountain of anger is critical to your ability to manage the complaint caller in an expert manner.

In order to do so, you must understand what fuels customer complaints and adjust your behavior accordingly. Your challenge is to help customers get down the other side of the mountain of anger without incident—making them feel comfortable, safe and secure. Isn't that what you expect when you're the dissatisfied customer?

Most customers believe they have good reason to complain, and there are many behind-the-scene factors that influence the customer's behavior. Seldom does the complaint caller become enraged during conversation—unless fuel has been added to the fire. Customers don't experience anger the minute they purchase your product or service. Mostly, the reason for the complaint is a direct result of something that has gone wrong. Perhaps, the customer is dissatisfied with the service provided by your company. Perhaps, the product purchased doesn't live up to customer expectations. There's any number of reasons why the dissatisfied customer exists.

Just remember, your customers go through several phases of behavior before and after climbing the mountain of anger. The best way for you to understand the emotions experienced by the disgruntled customer is to put yourself in the customer's place.

Use the following exercise to recall a time when you were the disgruntled customer.

Complaint Call Assessment

What caused you to become disgruntled? _____

_____

Which feelings did you experience? _____

_____

How many people did you tell and why? _____

_____

Did you complain? If so, to whom? _____

_____

How was your complaint call handled? _____

_____

What was the end result? _____

_____

Participants in our workshops and seminars share a variety of stories related to circumstances that cause them to climb the mountain of anger. Most people let their dissatisfaction be known. Some complaints find satisfactory resolution while others never do. Some people continue to be loyal, long-standing customers—others don't. Understandably, most everyone tells someone about their experience—positive or negative. Here's how the mountain of anger works.

Setting The Stage

Imagine that today is a very special day and you're excited. The surprise birthday party you planned for your daughter is at 7 p.m. and friends and family will all be there. What an important day. She's Sweet 16!

It's Saturday morning and you're called into work unexpectedly. No problem—the bakery is open until 6 p.m. You rush to the bakery on your way home, hurriedly pick up the birthday cake, drop it off at the recreation center, empty the party decorations from your trunk, dash home to grab a change of clothes and drive back to the recreation center to decorate the hall with friends. There isn't much time to spare—the guests will be arriving soon.

Everything looks great! Now you can place the birthday cake on the beautifully decorated table. You can't wait to see how it turned out! You open the box. You scream. The cake says "Happy 25th Wedding Anniversary, Jim and Dottie."

There's no doubt you're about to experience the thrill of climbing the mountain of anger.

Phase 1

You're appalled! Your surprise turns to anger! The bakery is closed! The guests are arriving. What will you do?

With anger in your voice and disappointment on your face, you explain to the guests that there's been a terrible mistake. You share your anger and frustration with everyone—30 teenagers and their parents. You didn't look at the cake before leaving the bakery, but you checked the inscription on the handwritten order form. You thought everything was fine. What will your daughter think. How embarrassing!

The room buzzes with excitement; your anger and dismay are contagious. Everyone rushes to your defense because they understand how you feel. You're eager to let the owner know about your dissatisfaction and vow never to do business with that bakery again!

Phase 2

You don't solicit input from the others—they just begin offering advice on how to handle the situation. One person says, "I'd demand a refund immediately." Another says, "The damage is done now. I'd write a letter to the business owner about how careless the employees are." Still another says, "Why write a letter? I'd just call the company up and give them a piece of my mind."

The advice keeps coming, and you appreciate it. It's comforting to know how concerned everyone is. Your anger has been validated—justified by the show of support you've received. You make a mental note of their comments before formulating a strategy for how to approach the bakery and what you'll say. You decide to call first thing Monday morning.

Meanwhile, you attempt to mask your anger in an effort to enjoy the party—you'll have all day Sunday to let your anger fester. But you can't stop thinking about the incident and neither can the others.

```
┌─────────────┐   ┌──────────┐         /\
│ ☺☺☺☺☺☺      │   │ You are  │        /  \
│ Supporters  │   │ here     │       / Mountain \
└─────────────┘   └──────────┘      /  of Anger  \
                                   /_____\
```

Phase 3

It's Monday. By now, you've recounted your story several times. You know exactly what you're going to say and how you'll say it. You place the call. Your supporters won't be disappointed. You begin your ascent up the mountain of anger. You rehearse your presentation again and again as you climb to the top.

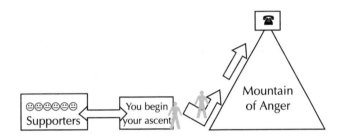

Phase 4

Someone sounding bright and cheerful answers your call. You ask to speak to the owner and learn that he's on vacation. You can't turn back now—you're proud of the presentation you've planned and have built up more anger throughout the weekend. Why should it go to waste? Someone needs to know what happened! Besides, you're not climbing the mountain alone—your supporters have played a major role in lifting you up the mountain. You know they're with you in spirit.

You begin telling your story: "I've never been so embarrassed in my life. You people made a mockery of my daughter's Sweet 16 birthday party!"

Can you identify this behavior style? _____

The service provider interrupts you with a defense against your attack, saying, "Calm down, lady. It's not my fault. I'm always careful to check the order against the inscription on the cake. I didn't do it and I don't know who did!"

Can you identify this behavior style? _____

The interruption instantly fuels your anger. You feel as though you're being pushed back down the mountain. You begin climbing to the top again, determined to deliver your complaint as practiced and planned.

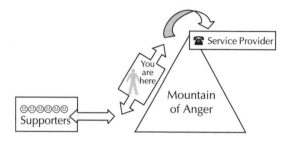

Phase 5

It's your turn now. You reach the top of the mountain again, this time pushing the service provider down the other side. You find it unacceptable that this person doesn't have the authority to resolve the problem. You want something to be done and you want it done now! You both continue to climb up and down the mountain—to no avail.

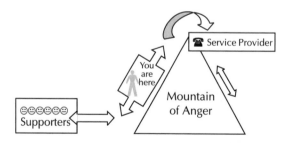

Each of you has generated a lot of energy during this call. Finally, you hang up the phone in disgust, wondering how the conversation could have gone more smoothly.

Phase 6

Fortunately—or unfortunately—the primary responsibility for handling the complaint caller in a professional manner rests with you.

The negative childlike and parental behavior styles demonstrated by the persons involved in this scenario aren't conducive to resolution. A demonstration of adult behavior by both parties would support a more positive outcome. You must keep in mind that parental behavior solicits childlike behavior and vice versa.

As a service provider, you must establish a personal complaint call strategy. This will enable you to recognize when you're positioned too near the top of the mountain of anger. In most instances, your customers want to vent their frustration—get it off their chest. When you're positioned at the top of the mountain there isn't enough leeway between the customer and the problem or between the problem and the solution. So someone's going to be knocked off the mountain!

Immediately adjust you attitude to demonstrate adult behavior and position yourself in the middle of the mountain; you don't want to be directly in the line of fire. This positioning gives you an opportunity to listen, be empathetic and demonstrate your problem-solving skills. From this perspective, you can become the bridge between customers and the problem—between the problem and the solution. You can play to win! You can help the customer down the mountain of anger comfortably, making them feel safe and secure and resolving their problem in a timely and efficient manner.

Imagine the complaint call being handled this way:

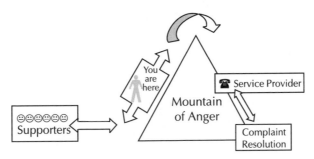

What are your observations and lessons learned from the mountain of anger? How will the ideal scenario help you improve your skills in handling the complaint caller?

List your observations and lessons learned.

1. _____

2. _____

3. _____

4. _____

5. _____

Complaint Call Strategy

Long-term customer loyalty and retention equal success for customer-driven organizations. It's imperative you develop a personal complaint call strategy. Take ownership of your ability to build a rapport, provide solutions and strengthen customer relationships.

We're typically caught off guard when confronted by complaint callers, and most situations are made worse when you "wing it." If you prepare yourself to manage customer relationships in adverse situations, the "mountain of anger" will no longer be an obstacle—but a "mountain to continued business success."

This six-step process assures your handling of complaint callers in a thoughtful considerate manner.

Step 1: Prepare Yourself

- Be knowledgeable about company policy
- Speak in a well-modulated vocal tone
- Don't personalize the caller's complaint
- Commit to the "adult behavior" style

Step 2: Listen-Up!

- Lend an empathetic ear
- Hear what's being said
- Provide productive feedback
- Make note of relevant details

Step 3: Establish a Rapport

- State your commitment to service excellence
- Obtain the caller's confidence
- Keep an open mind
- Ask questions to clarify key points

Step 4: Focus on Solutions

- Be realistic about the problem
- Use positive language
- Determine what will satisfy the caller
- Agree on a solution

Step 5: Summarize and Close

- Confirm the agreements you reach
- Express mutuality throughout the conversation
- Be specific about next steps
- Consider sending written confirmation

Step 6: Follow Through

- Keep your word
- Document all actions taken
- Keep the customer informed
- Make yourself available for follow-up

Friendly Reminders:

➤ Many complaint calls escalate because people hear what others say but they don't listen to understand what's being said.

➤ Establish a corporate commitment for positive, timely resolution of complaint calls.

➤ Avoid negative childlike and parental behaviors; adult behavior supports problem resolution.

➤ Placing yourself in the middle of the "mountain of anger" best positions you to listen and act responsibly.

Chapter 8

"Don't compromise yourself. You are all you've got."
– Betty Ford

Painting A Self-Portrait:
How Do Your Customers PICTURE You?

The most memorable gift we can give our customers is a positive first impression. Keep in mind that first impressions create lasting memories, whether they're positive or negative.

Most of us draw mental portraits of our customers or prospects on the telephone, often establishing long-term working relationships without ever meeting face-to-face. When we finally do meet, we're usually surprised their image doesn't match the portrait we painted of them. It seems we're quick to visualize the person on the other end of the telephone, never realizing they're visualizing us as well.

It's important to remember that your telephone communication doesn't offer the benefit of a friendly, firm handshake; smiles can't be seen; body language can't be read; and facial expressions can offer no clues. What you visualize depends upon what you hear. As a result, good telephone skills are necessary to paint a positive self-portrait for every customer.

Think about some of the characteristics that enable you to draw mental portraits of your customers. Think of a time when you experienced meeting a customer who didn't mirror the mental portrait you'd drawn of them. What were the major differences in perception?

My Portrait   **Actual**

_____   _____

_____   _____

_____   _____

_____   _____

Which characteristics influenced your perception?

_____   _____

_____   _____

_____   _____

Does your portrait reflect someone easygoing and laid back? How about someone who reminds you of an auctioneer because they talk too fast? Did you draw a portrait of someone who is strong and powerful, confident and in control? Or did you picture the customer as quiet, shy, meek and innocent? Does your portrait reflect someone who rambles or mumbles because you have difficulty understanding what's being said? Does your portrait bring to mind someone who may be extremely difficult and hard to please?

How do your customers see you? Do you demonstrate characteristics that create an image your customers will remember with pleasure? Do you project professionalism? Are you understandable? Do you give the impression you're willing to go the extra mile? Have you thought about how your physical posture, voice inflection, courteousness, vocal tone and rate of speech may influence the self-portrait you paint of yourself for the customer?

Imagine yourself as a valuable framed portrait—a real work of art! Step inside the framework of your image and visualize the customer's perception of you. Do you need to touch up a few rough images on the portrait before presenting yourself as a gift to your customer?

Using the word **PICTURE**, consider how the following characteristics can work to help you create a self-portrait everyone will remember with pleasure and won't be surprised to see.

P osture
I nflection
C ourtesy
T one
U nderstandability
R ate of Speech
E xtra Mile

Posture

When meeting someone face-to-face, posture and body language become very important characteristics. Why? Because people can see your stance, hand gestures and facial expressions. Your physical posture can help others know you're alert, confident and decisive.

When working with customers on the telephone, it's important you adopt the same posture you would if the caller were physically before you. Even though your customer can't see you, your telephone posture impacts the sound of your voice.

Be aware of "open" and "closed" postures. You want to give the impression you're fully alert—that you're paying close attention to what's being said. Folded arms and crossed legs can send a message of "closed" body language. Your customer may sense that you're not receptive to what's being said and may feel you've shut them out. Open up! Assume a comfortable position while seated—one that says, *I'm all ears and ready to help.*

It's difficult to mask our behavior through the sound of our voice. Make every effort to identify how your attitude impacts body language and vocal tone when talking with customers. Even though you think you're speaking tongue-in-cheek, the behaviors you demonstrate—while biting your tongue or talking through clenched teeth—can change your vocal tone and your negative attitude will be heard by the customer. Remember to put a smile in your voice, demonstrate a positive attitude and look good to yourself!

Don't let facial expressions and hand gestures give way to negativity. While talking with customers on the telephone, do you sometimes look as though you're posing for an aspirin commercial? A confused, worried or frustrated facial expression is likely to come through in your voice. Many of our workshop participants confess to rolling their eyes toward the ceiling, letting out a sigh of frustration or relief and turning their back on the customer. Do you have a tendency to "talk with you hands"—forgetting the person on the other end of the phone line can't see you? Do you fidget with gadgets on your desk, swivel in your chair or constantly tap your pencil when irritated?

When in a seated position, be certain your body is erect and that your chair is comfortable. You should be able to lean back in your chair 30 degrees. If you tend to lean back a lot while using the telephone, consider getting a neck rest. Make certain your telephone is positioned in an easy-to-reach place on the desk. If you consistently bend over or stretch out to retrieve files and other materials, your voice can sound strained and uncomfortable.

If you have difficulty maintaining good posture while being seated, stand up! Rather than slouch down in the chair or assume a position leaning over the desk—chin in hand—rise to the occasion. Speaking from a standing position allows you to breathe from your diaphragm. Assuming this position can be helpful if you're on a long call or need to renew your energy level.

Inflection

Use inflection to sound more personable and friendly. Sometimes it isn't so much what you say when talking with customers on the telephone, but how you say it. Use feeling in your voice to express an idea or a mood and speak in a manner that demonstrates a high energy level. You don't want to sound disinterested, boring or monotonous to the customer. Instead, speak to your customers as though they're a friend rather than an unwelcome visitor. Focus on demonstrating an ability to swing your voice up and down in a comfortable, natural, conversational tone.

Adding inflection to your voice helps you sound more friendly and conversational. Sometimes you sound robotic when you're accustomed to asking familiar questions or offering routine responses. Use inflection to emphasize key points in your conversation and as a tool for asking customer questions from a point of curiosity. You want to sound interested and concerned.

The average person spends only 3 to 6 seconds watching each station as they surf through numerous television channels because they're looking for something that sounds interesting. Imagine watching your favorite television show and hearing every actor speak in a dull, boring or monotonous voice. Chances are you'll lose interest in the program, change the channel and find another show that sounds more interesting. The actor's job is to keep you involved in his or her dialogue—to help you feel as though you're a part of their conversation.

You can practice using inflection by reading a paragraph from a book or magazine article and putting emphasis on key words. Here's a simple exercise that will help. Read the following paragraph aloud as though you're talking with your last customer of the day. Then read the paragraph again, as though you're talking with your best friend—saying that person's name before you begin each sentence.

> "The product you ordered is not currently in stock. I can place a back order for you unless you would prefer to call again after the first of the month. How would you like me to handle this?"

Observations:

(1) How did you sound when talking to the customer?

(2) Which words did you emphasize while talking with your "friend?"

(3) What difference did you notice in the sound of your voice?

1. _____

2. _____

3. _____

Be careful though, using inflection can send mixed messages to your customers, leaving them feeling discounted or puzzled by how you spoke to them. The inflection in your voice can change the entire meaning of your intended statement, resulting in miscommunication. Notice how the customer might translate the meaning of inflection in your voice:

Read each sentence aloud, putting emphasis on the highlighted word. As you read each statement, think about how the other person will feel. How will each statement be interpreted?

I think you misunderstood.
I **think** you misunderstood.
I think **you** misunderstood.
I think you **misunderstood.**

Observations:

(1) Which feelings or emotions are transmitted with each sentence?

(2) Was your message conveyed as you intended?

1. _____

2. _____

3. _____

4. _____

Courtesy

Always treat others the way you expect to be treated. Your customers know when you're genuinely interested in them and people respond in kind to people who are kind. When you put yourself in the customer's shoes, you're more likely to create a loyal, long-standing relationship.

You may not be a customer service representative, but one has certainly helped you. You may not be a waiter or waitress, but you certainly dine in restaurants. You may not be a government official, but you certainly encounter bureaucracy. You may not be a product sales person, but you purchase products from others. You may not be a corporate executive, but you understand the impact customer relationships have on a corporation's bottom line.

The point is that putting the shoe on the other foot can help you identify ways to apply the qualities and characteristics you value and appreciate most in your business dealings with others. You enjoy a healthy relationship with any service provider who is pleasant, understanding, helpful and considerate. Take a moment to identify the one person with whom you enjoy a wonderful business relationship.

Why is this person your favorite?

Which personality traits are most pleasant to you?

_____   _____

_____   _____

_____   _____

_____   _____

Review your list. Many of our workshop participants are surprised to discover the important role these characteristics play in a meaningful business relationship.

Which positive characteristics do you consistently demonstrate?

_____

_____

_____

_____

_____

_____

_____

Which characteristics can you improve upon?

_____

_____

_____

_____

Make every effort to project a positive, courteous image to reinforce your commitment to customer excellence. Use the following Courtesy Checklist as a friendly reminder to paint a positive self-portrait for every customer.

Courtesy Checklist

Give your customers more than they expect.
Demonstrate the following characteristics.

- ❑ Pleasant expression—Smile!
- ❑ Genuine interest and concern
- ❑ Sense of urgency
- ❑ Sincerity and integrity
- ❑ Pleasant attitude and personality
- ❑ Well-modulated voice and tone
- ❑ Look good to yourself
- ❑ Willingness to go the extra mile
- ❑ Sense of humor

Tone

Your vocal tone can set the stage for customer conversations on the telephone. It serves as an invaluable tool for establishing a rapport with others. It speaks volumes about your individuality and amplifies your attitude at that moment. Think about it: When you place calls to others, you can typically determine their mood by the tone of their voice.

Studies show that people speaking face-to-face convey messages through body language, tonality and actual word choice. These characteristics also impact our ability to communicate effectively on the telephone. Think carefully about how the following statistics would impact your ability to convey a message to your customer:

How Messages Are Conveyed

	Face-To-Face		Telephone
Body Language	55% _____%		_____%
Tonality	38% _____%		_____%
Actual Words	7% _____%		_____%

Contrary to popular belief, the percentage of a message conveyed through body language on the telephone is not zero! As we've discussed, your telephone posture affects your body language. Since your customers can't see you over the telephone, this percentage will be lower. How much it will decrease can depend on how your body language or posture affects the tone of your voice and the actual words you use.

Because you and the customer only have your audible senses at work, your vocal tone will have a significant impact on how you convey your message. You can expect the percentage for tonality to increase by as much as 86% when talking on the telephone with your customers.

The actual words you use to convey a message to customers on the telephone can increase to between 14% and 20%. It's important you choose your words carefully and deliberately. Add some variety to your pitch by using inflection to emphasize key words or phrases. Your customers may not remember everything you say, but they won't forget how you say it.

Voice Patterns

Your voice needs to sound professional, yet pleasant. Your customers will react not only to your vocal tone, but, in most instances, they'll mirror it.

Everyone wants to speak in a manner that gets and holds others' attention. Physiologically speaking, the positioning of your head can determine vocal tone. The angle in which you hold your head affects the air going through the voice box, creating either an approachable or a credible voice pattern.

In our effort to "speak with authority," we can often sound too serious, cold or unfriendly. It's difficult to project a smile in your voice when speaking in a tone that's unnaturally low—the voice used when you really mean business. On the other hand, some of us feel others don't take us seriously when we speak in a high-pitched voice—the voice used when you're excited, happy or cheerful. Is your natural vocal tone approachable or credible? Consider how becoming more aware of each voice pattern can positively impact your purpose or outcome.

Approachable voice. When you sound warm and friendly, your ability to establish a rapport with customers can increase significantly. Make every effort to speak in an approachable vocal tone—one that demonstrates your desire to establish a long-term, loyal relationship with customers.

If you're seeking information from a customer, the approachable vocal tone will serve you well. The following characteristics can determine an approachable voice pattern:

▶ *Head* typically bobs up and down, as though in agreement or affirming an understanding.

Position: ↕

▶ *Vocal Tone* is generally rhythmic, as demonstrated when using inflection.

Position: ⌇

▶ *Chin* typically curls up, as though to maintain eye contact or seek agreement of understanding.

Position: ⌐↑

Credible voice. The credible voice conveys confidence, competence and sophistication. We use this vocal tone when we speak with authority. If your vocal tone is naturally low, you'll experience little difficulty putting a smile in your voice.

If you're giving information in the conversation, the credible vocal tone will serve you well. The following characteristics can determine a credible voice pattern:

▶ *Head* typically still, as though little movement is required to signal agreement or affirmation.

Position: ▮

▶ *Vocal Tone* is generally flat, as demonstrated when speaking in a stern, matter-of-fact voice.

Position: ↔

▶ *Chin* typically curls down, as though signaling finality to every phrase.

Position: ⌐↓

Most people utilize a combination of approachable and credible voice patterns. Be aware of how each vocal tone impacts the outcome of your conversation. Pay particular attention to your natural voice pattern and focus on your expected outcome or purpose. Work to create balance of intonation as you communicate with your customers.

Understand the difference between an approachable voice and a credible one by doing this exercise.

Approachable and Credible Voice Patterns

1. Using an approachable voice pattern, say the first phrase of the sentence below—nod your head slightly, use inflection and curl your chin upward (⬆) at the end.

2. Repeat the first phrase using a credible voice pattern—keeping your head still, voice flat and then lowering your chin (⬎) as you say the word at the end of the statement.

3. Do this exercise for each of the next two phrases, paying close attention to the change in your vocal tone as you move from an approachable voice pattern to a credible one.

4. Finally, say the entire sentence in a conversational tone, being careful to notice which voice pattern seems to be more comfortable or natural for you.

Phrase one	Phrase two	Phrase three
Thank you for your order.	*We will process it now*	*so you can use the account today.*

"Understandability"

It's normal to think that everything you say is understandable; but how often do you really listen to yourself? How do you sound on the telephone to customers?
Your self-portrait needs to depict someone whose enunciation, diction, pronunciation and dialect is clear and easy to understand. You don't want to be caught mumbling, bumbling or rambling while talking on the telephone with your customers. And you shouldn't need to repeat yourself frequently during the course of a conversation.

One way to assess your own "understandability" is to recognize how often customers ask you to repeat what you've said. Create a mental "red flag" that will alert you each time this occurs then make a conscientious effort to recognize why they had trouble understanding you. Each of the friendly reminders that follow should cause your "red flag" to go up. File this information away for future reference to ensure you can manage improvement in every area.

Simple Basics

I'm appalled at what I often see when I visit companies throughout the United States. I've witnessed people talking with customers on the telephone while sipping from a coffee cup, water bottle or juice jar. I've seen eraser tips, straws, paperclips and ink pen caps dangling from the lips of service providers. I've seen people eating candy bars, potato chips, sandwiches and cookies. I've even witnessed one service provider asking the customer to "hold on a second" while licking an ice cream cone!

It's imperative you avoid talking with anything in or near your mouth. Your customer needs to have your undivided attention while conducting business over the telephone and anything less is unacceptable.

Pronunciation/Enunciation

Correct word pronunciation and enunciation is important when talking with customers on the telephone. Experts estimate there are more than 500,000 words in the English language. Your challenge: To be certain you're using correct pronunciation, grammar and word choice.

Make every effort to articulate your thoughts clearly and succinctly. Mispronouncing words can be embarrassing, especially if you're unaware of the correct pronunciation. If you don't know how to pronounce a particular word, look it up in the dictionary, and make a habit to practice saying the word correctly. Most customers won't correct your word usage—they'll snicker behind your back instead.

I met a young man who was eager to let me know how "flustrated" he was in his current work environment. Should I have corrected his word usage from "flustrated" to "frustrated?" Think about how you would feel if a customer did that to you.

Below are some of the most frequently mispronounced words: Do these sound familiar?

Incorrect	Correct
Wiff	With
Picher	Picture
Aks	Ask
Probly	Probably
Recanize	Recognize
Sumphen	Something

Diction

Remember that you're drawing a self-portrait of yourself for the customer. You want to appear confident and professional—not haphazard and unintelligible. Words run together when you don't enunciate each word clearly. What kind of mental portrait do you see when you hear the following phrases?

How cani help you?	Didn'tcha get the package yet?
I wanna be sure that...	I shudda called sooner, but...
Lemme call you back.	Wouldja complete this form?
I'm gonna talk to her taday.	What cani do feryou?

Other Considerations

It's easy to assume everyone understands your intercompany or industry lingo. Avoid speaking in acronym-eese without first stating what the acronym represents. Don't use slang when speaking with customers, for example: saying 24-7 when you mean 24 hours a day, seven days a week. Also, if you speak with an accent or geographical dialect, remember to speak slowly and be prepared to pronounce words phonetically or spell them for customers when necessary.

Rate Of Speech

Fast talkers are marveled at—but not heard! Your self-portrait shouldn't reflect an image of someone who speaks faster than a speeding bullet. Your rate of speech should be well-paced and easy to understand. The average person speaks at the rate of 120 to 130 words per minute. Sometimes we have a tendency to speak too fast—between 150 to 180 words per minute.

If you're a fast-talker, make a conscious effort to practice slowing your rate of speech. Think how you feel when the customer speaks too fast. Typically, you can ask the person to slow down, offering various reasons why they should—"I'm taking notes," or "I want to be certain I hear every detail."

Perhaps, you take special care to slowly process your thoughts with the intent of speaking deliberately. Slow talkers are often viewed as indecisive instead of pensive. Speaking too slowly can divert the listener's attention. Be careful to speak at a rate that helps the conversation flow—eliminate the frustration of customers or service providers who may feel like pulling the words from your mouth.

Be aware that a slow talker often irritates a listener because there's no way for the customer to ask you to speak faster. Think about how you feel when a customer speaks too slowly. Unlike the fast talker, you don't dare say, "Can you speed it up, pal? I've got other customers to deal with."

> If you speak too fast, use pauses to slow your rate of speech and make certain to enunciate your words clearly and succinctly. To slow your speech rate, subtract ten seconds from the length of time it takes to read this paragraph. To increase your speech rate, add ten seconds to your reading time. Determine a comfortable speech rate by reading this paragraph several times.

Extra Mile

It's important to remember that customer perception determines quality service. Most companies provide good customer service, but that's not enough! In today's competitive environment, you must provide excellent customer service. Going the extra mile for your customers means more than meeting their expectations—your challenge is to exceed them!

It's been said that the difference between "good" and "excellent" customer service is initiative. Take the initiative to go the extra mile for your customers. Look for opportunities to make a significant difference in their perception of you and your company. As a first step, review the Courtesy Checklist as well as the reasons you enjoy working with a particular person. Then make sure you're not overlooking the little things that can enhance your business relationships.

Use the following exercise to evaluate how you interact with customers.

Extra! Extra! Read All About It!

Answer this question: How would my actions appear if they were described on the front page of tomorrow's local newspaper?

_____

_____

_____

_____

What actions could I have taken to go the extra mile for this customer?

_____

_____

_____

_____

_____

Speaking Your Customer's Language

It's important to remember that most people use a combination of communication styles while speaking with others and each person has preferences as to how he or she relates to the world. You can identify a customer's listening language by paying close attention to the words he or she uses while speaking. In order to match their communication style, you can learn to use the same or similar words in response.

Once you identify your customer's preferred communication style, you'll know that what you mean to say is exactly what the customer hears and reacts to. Understanding predominant communication styles can increase the likelihood that the message you send will equal the message the other person receives.

People who communicate effectively learn the value of three predominate communication styles: Visual... Auditory... Kinesthetic.

Visual

Visually oriented people typically learn by seeing how something is done. They listen to you speak and visualize what you're saying. They tend to communicate by utilizing words that depict the visual elements of their world.

Examples of visual word usage are:

Do you see what I'm saying?
I can't imagine you don't understand our focus for this project.
Look at it this way.
I can't picture him as our new boss.
Let me show you what I mean.

Sometimes it's difficult to understand why the other person can't see your pictures—why they view things differently than you. Perhaps, the person to whom you're speaking isn't visual; you may be speaking with someone who is auditory or kinesthetic and, therefore, is not getting the visual you're giving.

Imagine your best friend invites you to attend a concert featuring a well-known rock band. You eagerly accept the invitation saying, "I haven't seen that group in years! I wonder how they look now." You're most likely going to the concert to see the rock band.

Auditory

People whose preferred communication style is auditory typically process information by just listening to what you say. They only need to hear how to do it; they don't need to see every detail in order to get the whole picture, and they tend to be bottom-line oriented. Those who are predominantly auditory communicate by utilizing words that amplify the auditory elements of their world.

Examples of auditory word usage are:

Do you hear what I'm saying?
I want to voice my opinion.
Listen to it this way.
I tune out when you don't sound interesting.
Let me tell you what I mean.

Sometimes it is difficult to understand why your comments don't click with the other person—why they hear things differently than you do. Perhaps, the person you're speaking to is not auditory; you may be speaking with someone who is kinesthetic or visual and, therefore, is not hearing what you're saying.

Imagine your best friend invites you to attend a concert featuring a well-known rock band. You eagerly accept the invitation saying, "I haven't heard that band in years! I'll bet they still sound good, too." You're most likely going to the concert to hear the band.

Kinesthetic

The kinesthetic person typically demonstrates a strong preference toward feeling the emotion of your words. Sometimes they can appear to be overly sensitive, but this isn't necessarily the case; they simply want to make certain you understand how they feel. They relate best when you point out things that can help them learn; they're hands-on listeners, and what you say will impact them in a special way. Those who are predominantly kinesthetic communicate by utilizing words that enable them to interact with the elements of their world.

Examples of kinesthetic word usage are:

> *I feel the same way you do about this.*
> *I don't handle rejection very well.*
> *I'm comfortable with our decision.*
> *The impact of your actions can be devastating.*
> *I need to get through all the clutter on my desk.*

Sometimes it's difficult for the other person to understand why your feelings are so important; they appear indifferent to your emotions. Perhaps, the person you're speaking to isn't kinesthetic. You may be speaking with someone who is visual or auditory and, therefore, is not sensing what you're feeling.

Imagine your best friend invites you to attend a concert featuring a well-know rock band. You eagerly accept the invitation saying, "I can handle that! Their music still makes me feel like dancing." You're most likely going to the concert to feel the music of the band.

Identifying Communication Styles

Your ability to develop skills that enable you to identify preferred communication styles has many advantages in your professional work environment. Once learned, these skills are transferable and can enhance your personal communication as well. Imagine becoming a better communicator with your family, friends and acquaintances.

With practice, you can identify the customer's preferred communication style by listening for word clues. Keep in mind that most of us have a communication preference and we let others know by the frequent use of words common to a specific communication style. Remember, however, that most of us utilize a combination of communication styles.

Here's a sampling of frequently used words in each of the three communication styles. Make a copy of this word list and checkmark the words you frequently use in conversation.

Can you identify your communication style?   _____ Visual   _____ Auditory   _____ Kinesthetic

Communication Styles Word List

Visual

Look	Picture	Illustrate	View
Sight	Clarify	Resemble	Paint
Draw	Focus	Show	Design
Imagine	See	Visualize	Depict

Auditory

Echo	Ring	Say	Ask
Click	Sing	Voice	Listen
Loud	Tell	Speak	Noise
Sound	Hear	Tune	Verbal

Kinesthetic

Get	Sensitive	Comfortable	Impact
Interact	Concern	Help	Stroke
Impress	Follow	Demonstrate	Handle
Relate	Grasp	Touch	Feel

The following exercise was inspired by the communication challenge experienced by one of our workshop participants. Identify the preferred communication styles (kinesthetic, visual, auditory) for each of the following scenarios, then circle the words that lead to your conclusion.

Communication Challenge

Naomi is an art instructor for a local community college. She sees her greatest challenge as getting students to view artwork through her eyes. Naomi struggles with how to illustrate the artist's ability to depict vibrant colors, beautiful flowers, landscapes and people. Some of her students, however, don't focus on the same images she does. It's like they can't look at the artwork and show their appreciation for what she sees.

Communication Style _____

When Naomi asked Jim how she could clarify the artist's concept for him, she was confused by his response. "I just don't seem to hear all you say with regard to comments about scenery. It sounds like you want me to see the harmony between the flowers, colors and landscape. That's difficult for me. So, I tune you out and begin amplifying the sounds in my mind of the summer breeze or focus on the ocean roaring in the background. I even hear the people talking. That's the only way it clicks for me."

Communication Style _____

Naomi became more concerned about her ability to effectively communicate when she saw that Amber didn't get the picture either. Amber explained, "I'm impressed with the interaction of the people in painting. I relate better and feel more comfortable getting in touch with the artist when I can filter through all the clutter on canvass. When you point out different images in the artwork, the impact of what the artist is demonstrating really hits home. Then, I finally get it."

Communication Style _____

It seems Naomi has a lot to learn about preferred communication styles. What can she do to help students see her point of view?

_____

_____

_____

_____

Matching Communication Styles

Think how effective customer communication can be when you learn to match your communication output to how others input information. With practice, you can tailor your communication style to match every customer interaction—without the need to change your own preferred style of communicating. Your challenge is learning to comfortably and naturally switch from one style to another in order to assure communication occurs. Here's an example of how it works:

Customer: *I can't see why the actual product looks so much different than the picture in your catalogue.*

You: *You're right! The picture in our catalogue shows a different view of the model you looked at last month.*

In this example, you've successfully matched the customer's preferred communication style. You wouldn't say:

*It sounds like you didn't hear me say
there would be a slight difference between the two.*

Here's your chance to practice matching! First check out the following example.

Customer: *I can't seem to grasp the impact your new billing system will have on our company. Perhaps, you can demonstrate how it fits with our current system.*

Response: *I understand how you feel. Perhaps, you'll be more comfortable knowing that the impact will be minimal. The two systems will interact in a similar manner.*

Communication Style ____Kinesthetic____

Now you try. Write a response switching from one style to another using visual, auditory and kinesthetic, respectfully. Refer to the Words Typically Used In Specific Communication Styles list to identify each response. Then circle the words in your response that identify each preferred communication style.

You: _____

_____

_____

Communication Style _____

You:

_____

_____

_____

Communication Style _____

You:

_____

_____

_____

Communication Style _____

Learning to recognize the three preferred communication styles will enable you to provide better customer service. Your communication will be more understandable and relevant when you match your response style to that of your customers. Learn to recognize how your customer sees, hears, and feels.

Friendly Reminders:

➤ There are three preferred communication styles: Visual... Auditory... Kinesthetic.

➤ Determine your preferred style of communication.

➤ Identify your customer's preferred style of communication.

➤ Listen for key words in your customer's vocabulary so you can customize your response.

➤ Practice matching preferred communication styles with customers, family and friends.

Chapter 10

"You can make more friends in two months by becoming interested in other people than you can in two years by trying to get people interested in you."
– Dale Carnegie

Now Hear This:
Hearing Is Not Listening!

Companies lose millions of dollars every year because of miscommunications resulting from failure to listen to and understand customers' needs. Improving your listening skills is essential if your intent is to provide quality customer service. The more you demonstrate an interest in customers, the more you know about them and what they need. Listening is an art that improves with practice. It stands to reason that the more you learn about your customers, the better you can serve them. You can even help your customers become better listeners.

Numerous university studies have shown that most of us demonstrate a very low rate of listening effectiveness. The average American listens at an effective rate of only 25%. If you're like most people, your immediate recall of a brief message of average length is only 50%, which is typically reduced to 25% within 48 hours. Because you have only your audible senses at work, this percentage can drop even lower if the brief message was received via the telephone.

Remember that your customers can't see you through the telephone. You don't have the advantage of using visual input to effectively communicate your message and neither do they. Many people confuse hearing with listening. Just because you hear the customer's words doesn't necessarily mean you're listening to their message. Why? Because distractions tend to break our concentration. And instead of listening to what's being said, many of us are already listening to what we're going to say.

Work to improve your skills for active listening, identify barriers to listening and utilize techniques that can help the customer listen to you.

Ten Tips For Active Listening

Prepare to Listen

Preparing yourself to listen is an active process. A long-time friend used to say, "I need to stay ready to keep from getting ready." If you aren't prepared to listen, you aren't prepared to transact business with the customer on behalf of your company. Here are some ways to prepare to listen:

◆   Know your company's products and services well enough to be able to field customer questions, redirect calls or make appropriate referrals when necessary.

◆   Arrange your office so desk accessories are placed where items used most are closest to you and make sure to keep pen and paper handy. Nothing challenges your organizational integrity more quickly than when you say, "Let me get something to write with," or "Wait a second, I need to find a piece of paper to write on."

◆   Opposites do attract! Organize your desk in a way that gives easier access to essential communication tools. If you're right-handed, place the telephone on the left side of your desk and writing utensils on the right. This way, you can pick up the telephone receiver with the left hand and be ready to write with the opposite one. Reverse the arrangement if you're left-handed. This may seem a bit awkward at first, but you'll be surprised at how well it works.

◆ Give the customer your undivided attention. Stop whatever you're doing before you pick up the telephone receiver. If you're working on the computer, remove your free hand from the keyboard or take your hand off the mouse! Avoid continuing to focus your attention on previous work and shift your focus to the person on the other end of the phone line.

◆ When placing an outbound call, prepare notes and questions in advance. Organize your thoughts in an effort to free your mind for listening.

Focus on the Customer—Not Yourself!

What you learn from active listening will help you understand what the customer's real needs are—and how your product or service addresses them. You're more likely to exceed the expectations of customers if you keep their interests and viewpoints in mind. It's easy to become impatient with a caller when you think you understand their point before they finish telling you what it is. Put yourself in the customer's shoes and make every effort to remain open and receptive to what's being said.

There's an old adage: When a customer goes into a hardware store looking for a drill or a drill bit, what he really wants is a hole. Make certain you listen to understand what kind of holes your customers want so you can provide the service they need.

There are standard responses and solutions for nearly every situation. Don't take the easy way out. Listen for ideas that provide opportunities to be creative in developing positive customer responses. Think about how you can tailor solutions to make customers feel special. You want your company to stand head and shoulders above the rest. The following phrases show you're listening:

Now that I know you like desert flowers, perhaps a southwestern pattern would work best.

A spin-off from your perception of the floor plan might be to add more space in the kitchen area.

You've just given me an idea! What would you think about...?

Know When to Interrupt

Contrary to popular belief, you can't talk and listen at the same time. There's a reason why you have two ears and only one mouth. Your objective is to serve the customer well and you can't accomplish this goal unless you listen to what customers say. If you're doing more than half of the talking, then you're only doing half of the listening. Learn to listen twice as much as you speak.

Though what you have to say is important, resist the urge to interject your thoughts while the customer is speaking. The conversation will flow a lot smoother if you realize that the quickest way to get an abundance of information is to let the customer talk without interruption. Make a conscious effort to allow adequate time for relevant facts to surface and avoid interrupting for the sake of having your say. Instead, become a partner in the information exchange.

Of course, there will be times when the conversation gets off track and you may need to interrupt the customer. When such instances occur, wait for a pause that signals the customer has completed a particular train of thought. Then obtain permission to interrupt. Use outlining skills to help focus the customer's attention on the point(s) you wish to make. You might say:

> *(pause) May I interrupt, Ms. Crawford?*
> *If I understand you correctly, your request is regarding points a, b and c of the contract.*

> *(pause) Please excuse the interruption, Crystal. The way I understand it is....*

> *(pause) Mr. Carson, may I interrupt at this point?*
> *I want to make certain I understand your concerns about....*

Using outlining skills during conversation is a great way to avoid miscommunication. It gives you a chance to let the customer know you're actively listening so you'll understand what's being said.

Use Listening Responses

While you don't want to interrupt the customer needlessly, you do want to let them know you're focused on what's being said. The customer will appreciate your thoughtfulness and attentiveness when you use these techniques to demonstrate interest, empathy and understanding.

◆ Offer thoughtful, low-level responses to show your interest in the conversation. Use phrases like "I understand," "Yes," "That's sounds interesting" or "What happened next?"

◆ An occasional affirmation can demonstrate your empathy for the customer's reason for calling. Use phrases like "I know what you mean," "I understand how you feel" or "I see your point."

◆ Reflect upon previous comments to acknowledge your understanding and to assure the customer that you're paying attention. Rephrase what the customer has said to make sure that what you heard is exactly what was said and meant.

You might say:

> *When you described the imperfection, you said....*
> *As you pointed out earlier in the conversation....*
> *You mentioned that....*
> *I agree with your observation that....*
> *I understand how you feel when you say....*

Avoid Being Judgmental

Remember that you're opening yourself up for judgment by the manner in which you handle every call. You want to paint a self-portrait that projects a professional image and reflects positively on you and your company, so focus on substance rather than the manner in which customers present themselves for view.

You'll undoubtedly encounter many personalities and attitudes when working with customers on the telephone. You will hear fast and slow talkers, friendly and angry customers, people with dialects, accents and speech impediments. Your challenge is to listen—not look! Avoid spending time drawing mental portraits of the customer and pay close attention to what's being said.

Be mindful of your tendency to develop preconceived notions about the customer and avoid formulating negative images that may impact your attitude. You can run the risk of responding and reacting differently than usual when you're preoccupied with the mental portrait you've drawn.

Listen Between the Lines

You can often read feelings between the lines and can learn more about the customer from the way things are said and the manner in which they react to the things you say.

Listen carefully to the customer's vocal tone, voice pattern, inflection and pause pattern for clues that may help you understand the customer's feelings throughout the conversation. Remember that our voices project a variety of emotions, including warmth, sincerity, anxiety, understanding, confusion, impatience, interest and concern. Dramatic changes in pitch, tone, volume, inflection and rate of speech could signal a problem.

Make every effort to identify the customer's preferred communication style as you listen closely to what's being said. Is this person predominantly visual, auditory or kinesthetic? Guarantee effective communication by listening for word clues that will help you match an individual's communication style.

Concentrate

One of the most challenging aspects of active listening is your ability to concentrate on what's being said. Remember that the average person speaks at a rate of 120 to 130 words per minute; however, most of us can listen and think at a rate of 600 to 800 words per minute. This is the reason you can easily focus on other things while in conversation with a customer on the telephone.

Have you ever been talking to a customer and suddenly wondered if you closed the garage door before you left home? You mentally step outside of the conversation to retrace your tracks, recalling circumstances that will help you remember if the garage door was left open. Meanwhile, you maintain that you're really listening to the customer and pretend to have heard every word that was said. Once you reconnect with the conversation, you're likely to have missed an important point or comment, causing you to ask, "What did you say?"

You can easily be distracted by passersby, street noises, office chatter, loud talk, music, etc. Make a conscious effort to block out distractions and focus your mind on what's being said. You might find it helpful to lower your eyes (and in some instances you may need to lower your head) to divert your attention away from outside influences in order to focus on the conversation.

Concentrate on being in the moment and avoid listening ahead. You'll hear little or nothing if you're too busy thinking about what you're going to say next or contemplating the customer's next comment.

Stay Calm

Whatever happens during the call, you don't want to lose your composure. Make every effort to remain calm when interacting with customers on the phone. Keep clear objectives in mind and maintain an outward expression of neutrality. Remember that a negative attitude can often be heard in your voice and will certainly interfere with the listening process. These tips can help you stay calm during stormy encounters:

◆ Take a deep breath. Count to ten if you must, but breathe evenly and naturally!

◆ Demonstrate adult behavior and remember to let your positive attitude control conditions rather than letting conditions control your attitude. Avoid demonstrations of negative childlike and parental behavior!

◆ Be mindful of the impact posture and body language have on your vocal tone and attitude (no foot shaking, finger pointing or arm waiving). Maintain a physical posture that demonstrates open body language (no folded arms, crossed legs or hands on hip). You still need to hear the customer out—be receptive!

◆ Be aware of the impact facial expressions have on your attitude (no rolling your eyes, wrinkling your forehead or wearing a frown). Don't tune the customer out!

◆ Remember the mountain of anger. Position yourself half-way down the mountain allowing enough leeway for you to listen patiently to what's being said. Avoid climbing up and down the mountain.

◆ Speak in a conversational tone. Be certain to use inflection in an expression of empathy, not sarcasm. Remember, it's not so much what you say but how you say it.

Fill in the Knowledge Gaps

Few of us are experts about every topic that will arise. Use customer conversations to learn more about the person you're dealing with and to gain insightful information that will help you deliver quality customer service. Be certain to provide listening opportunities for the customer; they may need to know more than "How much does it cost?" and "When it will be delivered?"

These tips will help you fill in the knowledge gaps:

◆   Invite questions throughout the conversation. Many times our explanations aren't clear to the customer. Answer questions truthfully and be patient and respectful when you respond.

◆   As you listen to the facts, ask yourself which are most important? What is the main idea here? Is this situation similar to anything I have already experienced? Do I have all the information I need to service this customer properly?

◆   Ask relevant, productive questions that solicit specific information. Do you require more clarity? Do you need to uncover problems? Do you need to confirm an agreement or get consensus? Do you need to learn about buying decisions and objections? Do you need to qualify a prospect?

Take Notes

Avoid the mistake of trying to remember everything that's said. When you take notes, your retention rate can increase as much as 50%. When you talk about what you've heard or learned, retention can increase as much as 75%. Take notes to help you remember important information, but don't try to get all the details down on paper. If you focus more on writing lengthy documentation, you're likely not to pay full attention to what's being said. Jot down key phrases or words, names, numbers—just enough information to help you summarize the conversation.

Don't just file your notes away. Use them to understand expectations and follow-up activities. Repeat and verify key points and solicit feedback from the customer. Doing so will make communication much more accurate and effective.

Five Common Barriers To Listening

Most all of us have at least one thing in common when it comes to active listening. Here are some negative listening habits that keep us from hearing what's being said:

We Think We Already Know

When you think you already know something, there's no reason for you to absorb additional information. Your continued professional and personal growth and development are dependent upon increasing your knowledge base.

Psychologists have found that the more convinced we are of our knowledge, the wider the gap between what we really know and what we think we know. In one experiment, people were asked which is longer, the Panama Canal or the Suez Canal; then they were asked how sure they were about their response. Those who were 90% certain, were only 65% right. Those who were 60% certain, were only 50% right.

You don't want to earn a reputation as a know-it-all, so listen with the intent of gaining new insights from every customer interaction.

Jumping to Conclusions

A good communicator is a good listener. Make every effort to hear everything your customers have to say. You can improve your chances for achieving active listening success when you keep these tips in mind:

◆   Avoid the tendency to derail conversations. Changing the subject too quickly lets the customer know you're not interested in what they have to say.

◆   Avoid putting words in the customer's mouth or finishing their sentences for them.

◆   Avoid listening ahead, making assumptions about what you think the customer is going to say.

◆   Listen carefully to make certain the customer has finished speaking—a brief pause doesn't necessarily signal an end to the customer's conversation.

Daydreaming

Learn to concentrate and block out distractions. Drifting off during conversation can lead to an embarrassing "Can you repeat that?" or "I didn't hear what you said."

If trying to focus or concentrate on the conversation is challenging for you, find a place within the work area that is more conducive to listening. Consider rearranging your office furniture so your desk doesn't face the flow of traffic. And if all else fails, close the door to your office or create a "do not disturb sign" for your cubicle.

Preferential Bias

In most instances, we hear only what we want to hear. When you develop preferences you may tend to misinterpret new information to support those preferences, which can often cause you to pay little attention to other information that doesn't support your preference.

It's easy to discount customer opinion when you respond too quickly to what has been said without thinking about the consequences for your actions. Avoid challenging everything the customer says based on your personal interpretations. Remember to keep an open mind during customer conversations. When you get sidetracked making mental comparisons or unwarranted assessments about the customer's opinions, you can miss important details or relevant information.

Lack of Practice

It's not surprising that most of us demonstrate poor listening skills. Hearing what others say occurs involuntarily; but listening to understand what's being said is an art. Confucius said it best in 451 BC: "What I see, I remember. What I hear, I forget. But what I do, I understand."

In order to change your listening behavior, you must continually practice new techniques. Make active listening a priority in your life. Commit to making beneficial behavioral changes that will help improve your listening skills. Practice one active listening technique per week until you're confident you've become the best listener you can be.

Which three listening skills do you need to improve?

1. _____

2. _____

3. _____

Encouraging Customers To Listen

Miscommunication can occur whenever you notice the customer isn't paying full attention to what you're saying. Make listening a dual responsibility between you and the customer. Use these tips to encourage your customers to listen attentively:

◆ Chances are you can recall several occasions when you got far more information than you needed. Respect the customer's listening time. Be brief, concise and to the point when possible. If there is a simple answer to the customer's question, provide it and avoid giving unnecessary details that are irrelevant to the customer's request.

◆ Personalize the conversation by mentioning the customer's name when making important points. Use their name as an attention grabber when you have something really interesting to say, for instance:

> *Please remember, Mary, the doctor will be working from our downtown office that day.*

◆ Perhaps, the customer is experiencing distractions that make it difficult to concentrate on what you're saying. It's often helpful when you emphasize key points by using inflection and pauses.

◆ Encourage note taking. A tactful way of encouraging your customers to take notes is to explain that the information may be a bit confusing, or that you have several points to discuss and it would be helpful if they could write down what you're about to say.

◆ Solicit customer feedback and comments. Ask the customer to repeat important details by saying, "Marjorie, I want to be sure I didn't leave anything out. Would you mind repeating the information I just gave you?"

In Summary

"If you are totally customer-focused and you deliver the services your customers want, everything else will follow."

– Roger A. Enrico

Communication Is The Key

I trust **Beyond "Hello"** met the objective of (1) offering a friendly reminder of the impact telephone communication can have on your bottom line and (2) providing new insights and practical, useful information that can help you improve your professional and interpersonal communication skills.

We're quick to judge how others manage telephone communication, but often don't evaluate our own personal communication skills. Let your recollection of how others treat you on the telephone serve as a framework for creating a positive image your customers will remember with pleasure. When you put yourself in the role of the customer you can understand how learning to use the telephone more effectively will strengthen and enhance your company's customer service and marketing efforts. You need to make telephone communication and quality customer service synonymous.

Everyone who experiences customer contact over the telephone can use the many tips, tricks and techniques found in **Beyond "Hello."** Commit to setting the highest standard of professional excellence to continuously improve your telephone interaction. Make time to review the fundamental skills necessary for successful telephone communication and get back to basics—there's always room for improvement!

Think about what you do that influences how the person on the other end of the line perceives you and how valuable first impressions become when communicating on the telephone:

◆   Do you transmit a positive image?

◆   Is your telephone attitude positive or negative?

◆   How are your skills in greeting, screening, probing, transferring, holding, taking messages and responding?

◆   Do you make the best use of your voice messaging system?

◆   Do you manage complaint callers as profit opportunities?

◆   Have you looked at your self-portrait lately?

◆   Are you speaking your customer's language?

◆   Have you worked diligently to become an active listener?

◆   Do you encourage customers to listen to you?

I can't resist the urge to offer you one more exercise—this is the last one—I promise. Which skills have you worked hard to develop, e.g., dancing, carpentry, drawing, skiing?

Name two skills you perform exceptionally well?

1. _____

2. _____

Which methods did you use to perfect these skills?

1. _____

2. _____

3. _____

4. _____

I probably wouldn't lose a dime if I bet you that you perfected these skills through practice. The same is true for improving your telephone communication skills—practice makes perfect!

Thanks for reading **Beyond "Hello."** The experience of providing you with a guide for excellent telephone communication and quality customer service is more rewarding than you can imagine. It's my hope that you'll share the concepts in this book with others. I've even included an order form for obtaining additional copies for your customers, employees, coworkers, friends and family. It only takes one person to initiate a positive change—imagine the possibilities. Together, we can impact telephone skills and customer service perceptions throughout America!

Jeannie Davis

Things To Remember

Chapter 1 - Attitude:
Now You Hear It–Now You Don't

_____

_____

_____

_____

_____

_____

_____

_____

_____

_____

_____

Chapter 2 - How To Say "Hello": Guidelines For Professional Greetings

_____

_____

_____

_____

_____

_____

_____

_____

_____

_____

_____

_____

Chapter 3 - Call Screening And Probing: Getting The Information You Need

_____

_____

_____

_____

_____

_____

_____

_____

_____

_____

_____

_____

Chapter 4 - Call Transfer And Holding: Handling Calls Like A Pro

_____

_____

_____

_____

_____

_____

_____

_____

_____

_____

_____

_____

_____

Chapter 5 - Messaging:
The Give And Take Of It

_____

_____

_____

_____

_____

_____

_____

_____

_____

_____

_____

_____

_____

Chapter 6 - Voice Messaging:
A Condiment For Business Success

_____

_____

_____

_____

_____

_____

_____

_____

_____

_____

_____

_____

_____

Chapter 7 - Handling Complaint Callers: Profit Opportunities With A Twist

Chapter 8 - Painting A Self-Portrait: How Do Your Customers PICTURE You?

_____

_____

_____

_____

_____

_____

_____

_____

_____

_____

_____

_____

_____

_____

Chapter 9 - Communication Styles: Speaking Your Customer's Language

_____

_____

_____

_____

_____

_____

_____

_____

_____

_____

_____

_____

Chapter 10 - Now Hear This:
Hearing Is Not Listening!

_____

_____

_____

_____

_____

_____

_____

_____

_____

_____

_____

_____

Now Hear This, Inc. Publishing

14571 E. Mississippi Avenue #213
Aurora, CO 80012

303-337-1991 ◆ 800-745-5525 ◆ (Fax) 303-337-1966

Order Form

Beyond "Hello": A Practical Guide For Excellent Telephone
Communication and Quality Customer Service

Quantity _____ x **$24.95** _____
CO Residents add 7.45% sales tax _____
Subtotal $ _____
Shipping & Handling($4.50/book) _____
($1.50 each additional book)

Total enclosed: $ _____
(allow up to 3 weeks for delivery)

❑ **Mastercard**   ❑ **Visa**   ❑ **Check**

Card Number: _____ Expiration: _____

Name (as it appears on card): _____

Signature: _____

Ship to: (Please print)

Name: _____

Phone: _____

Company: _____

Address: _____

City/State/Zip: _____

Call for Rates on Large Quantities or International Shipments

Send information about Jeannie's on-site "Telephone Imagery"

❑ **Workshops**   ❑ **Seminars**   ❑ **Keynote Presentations**